fresh Techniques for Rubber Stamped CARDS

A TweetyJill Publication by Jill Haglund

ACKNOWLEDGEMENTS

Copyright by TweetyJill Publications, Inc. 2008
First Edition
Fresh Techniques for Rubber Stamped Cards

Published and created by:
TweetyJill Publications, Inc.
5824 Bee Ridge Road, PMB 412 Sarasota, FL 34233
For information about wholesale, please contact customer service at
www.tweetyjill.com or 1-800-595-5497.

TweetyJill Publications, Inc. has taken every measure to ensure that all information in this book is accurate. In addition, since individual skill levels, tools and circumstances vary, we cannot be held responsible for any losses, injuries or damages that may result from using any information provided in this book.
Printed in China ISBN 978-1-891898-15-0

Book Layout:
Jill Haglund & Lindsay Haglund

Graphic Designer:
Laurie Doherty

Creative Director:
Jill Haglund

Managing Editor:
Lindsay Haglund

Photography: Herb Booth
of Herb Booth Studios, Inc.,
Sarasota, FL

Photo Stylists:
Jill Haglund & Lindsay Haglund

Table of Contents

Ferns, flowers and butterflies... these are some of our favorite rubber stamps to collect because of their beautiful designs. This chapter displays an elegant array of nature-themed cards using techniques such as applying bleach to stamps, stamping in polymer clay, mosaic art and much more. Whether you are a beginner or an experienced rubber stamper, you always have nature stamps on hand, so pick them up and get creative!

"Who's been painting my roses red?
Who's been painting my roses red?
Who dares to taint, with vulgar paint,
the royal flowerbed? For painting my
roses red...someone will lose his head!"

~ The Queen of Hearts,
   Alice in Wonderland by Lewis Carroll

Purple Bachelor Buttons
AMY WELLENSTEIN

MATERIALS

Rubber Stamps: Floral Document and Black & White (Script) by Stampington & Co.

Pigment Inkpads: ColorBox MetalExtra (Goldrush) by Clearsnap

Dye Inkpads: Adirondack (Pitch Black) by Ranger

Papers: Green, Purple and Black Cardstock; Watercolor Paper

Markers/Pens: Green, Blue, Purple and Brown Water-Based Markers

Adhesives: Glue Stick

Tools: Embossing Heat Tool; Water Bottle; Paper Cutter

TECHNIQUE
• *Faux Watercolor with Marker and Dye Ink*

INSTRUCTIONS

1. Color Floral Document stamp with markers as shown and rub Pitch Black ink along edge.
2. Lightly spritz inked stamp with water and press onto watercolor paper. Use heat tool to dry image.
3. Cut and mat artwork onto black cardstock.
4. Stamp Black & White (Script) in Goldrush, covering purple cardstock. Use heat tool to dry ink.
5. Cut and mat purple cardstock onto folded green card; adhere original artwork to card.

Elegant Stems
AMY WELLENSTEIN

MATERIALS

Rubber Stamps: Rose Print by Stampington & Co.

Dye Inkpads: Adirondack (Sepia and Butterscotch) by Ranger

Papers: Red Patterned Paper by 7gypsies for Autumn Leaves; Black and Brown Cardstock; Watercolor Paper

Markers/Pens: Red and Green Water-Based Markers

Adhesives: Glue Stick

Tools: Embossing Heat Tool; Water Bottle; Paper Cutter

TECHNIQUE
• *Faux Watercolor with Marker and Dye Ink*

INSTRUCTIONS

1. Apply Butterscotch and Sepia inks to text and patterned areas of stamp. Color flower and leaves with markers.
2. Lightly spritz inked stamp with water and press onto watercolor paper. Use heat tool to dry image.
3. Cut and mat artwork onto black cardstock and Red Patterned paper; adhere to folded brown card.

Dream of Love
MAGGIE CRAWFORD

MATERIALS

Rubber Stamps: Alphabet by Hero Arts; Script by Stampers Anonymous

Dye Inkpads: StâzOn (Jet Black) by Tsukineko

Papers: Black Cardstock; Love Paper by 7gypsies

Embellishments: Black Elastic String; Black Eyelets

Adhesives: Glue Stick; Tacky Glue; Tape

Other: Letter Stencil

Tools: 1/8" Hole Punch; Makeup Sponge; Eyelet Setting Tool; Scissors; Paper Cutter

TECHNIQUE
• *Collage with Stamps*

INSTRUCTIONS

1. Cut a rectangle of Love paper. Tear a strip of black card stock. Adhere both to black folded card as shown.
2. Stamp Script in Jet Black onto white cardstock.
3. Tape stencil in place and sponge black dye ink over exposed cardstock.
4. Remove stencil and cut and mat image onto black cardstock.
5. Trim small pieces of white cardstock and stamp phrase in Jet Black using Alphabet stamps.
6. Fold pieces as shown and punch holes for eyelet placement.
7. Set eyelets and string paper loops onto black elastic.
8. Wrap elastic around stamped panel, adhering in back.
9. Attach panel in center of card as shown.

Love Nature
MAGGIE CRAWFORD

MATERIALS

Rubber Stamps: Butterfly and Dragonfly by Hero Arts

Papers: Black Cardstock; Love Paper by 7gypsies

Embellishments: Black Slides; Black Gingham Ribbon

Adhesives: Glue Stick; Tacky Glue; Glue Dots by Glue Dots International

Tools: Scissors; Paper Cutter

TECHNIQUE
• *Stamping on Slides*

INSTRUCTIONS

1. Cut and mat Love paper onto folded black card.
2. Adhere black gingham ribbon along center of card.
3. Stamp Butterfly and Dragonfly in Jet Black onto slides as shown.
4. Adhere slides to card with Glue Dots.

Inspire, Dream, Love

MAGGIE CRAWFORD

MATERIALS

Rubber Stamps: Sunflower by Magenta; Bee and Leaves by A Stamp In The Hand; Sabal Branch by Fred Mullett; Butterfly Words by Stampa Rosa; "Inspire, Dream, Love" by Kathleene Callei for American Art Stamp

Pigment Inkpads: ColorBox PetalPoint (Arboretum) and ColorBox MetalExtra (Goldrush) by Clearsnap

Papers: Dark Green and White Cardstock

Markers/Pens: Gold Leafing Pen by Krylon

Adhesives: Glue Stick; Adhesive Foam Tape

Other: Post-It® Notes or Removable Tape

Tools: Stipple Brushes; Embossing Heat Tool; Paper Cutter

INSTRUCTIONS

1. Stipple white cardstock using orange and pink shades from the PetalPoint.
2. Stamp "Inspire, Dream, Love" in Goldrush over inked cardstock and set ink with heat tool.
3. Cut and mat artwork to folded dark green card.
4. Cut additional white cardstock into square sheet.
5. Use two Post-It® Notes to isolate top right quarter of sheet. Stipple this area with light green and stamp Bee in darker green on top.
6. Isolate another quarter of cardstock; stipple with light orange and stamp Sunflower on top in pink.
7. Continue with this method until all four quadrants are covered with art.
8. Outline stamped cardstock with Gold Leafing Pen.
9. Adhere square sheet with adhesive foam tape.

TIPS
- *How do you stipple*? Dab stipple brush in inkpad; using short quick motions, pounce brush onto cardstock. Apply lightly for soft colors and heavily for darker shades.

Butterfly

MAGGIE CRAWFORD

TECHNIQUES

- *Paper Masking*
- *Stipple Art*

INSTRUCTIONS

1. Cut white cardstock to desired size.
2. Use Post-It® Notes or removable tape to mask off each side of cardstock leaving a single exposed vertical strip.
3. Stipple area with purple from the PetalPoint and stamp Flower Border in dark purple on top.
4. Continue this card using the Paper Masking technique. Vary the size and shape of each isolated area. Stipple in light colors and stamp in darker shades.
5. Stamp "Inspire, Dream, Love" in Goldrush over several areas after other art is completed.
6. Set ink with heat tool and adhere to folded purple card.

Note: Giraffe card by Maggie Crawford is made using the Paper Masking and Stipple Art techniques.

MATERIALS

Rubber Stamps: Butterfly by JudiKins; Leaves by A Stamp In The Hand; Flower Border by Magenta; "Inspire, Dream, Love" by Kathleene Callei for American Art Stamp

Pigment Inkpads: ColorBox PetalPoint (Aurora) and ColorBox MetalExtra (Goldrush) by Clearsnap

Papers: Purple and White Cardstock

Adhesives: Glue Stick

Other: Post-It® Notes or Removable Tape

Tools: Stipple Brushes; Embossing Heat Tool; Paper Cutter

TIPS
- If you are working with a limited amount of ink colors, you can stipple and stamp in the same color. Stipple lightly and the stamped image will always appear darker.

Butterfly and Bee

MAGGIE CRAWFORD

MATERIALS

Rubber Stamps: Butterfly and Bee by JudiKins

Pigment Inkpads: VersaMark Watermark (Clear) by Tsukineko

Embossing Powders: Black

Papers: Black and Cream Cardstock

Adhesives: Glue Stick

Other: Undiluted Bleach

Tools: Blend and Flo Pen by Dove Brushes; Embossing Heat Tool; Paper Cutter

INSTRUCTIONS

1. Apply Clear ink to stamp and press onto black cardstock.
2. Cover image with black embossing powder and heat briefly without fully embossing the image.
3. Fill Blend and Flo Pen with freshly opened, undiluted bleach.
4. Paint image with bleach, being careful to stay within the embossed lines.
5. Heat image again, thoroughly embossing. This second application of heat enhances the bleach.
6. For additional color go back over small areas with Blend and Flo Pen.
7. Cut and mat artwork onto cream cardstock; adhere to folded black card.

TIPS

- Bleach must be freshly opened for this technique to work properly.
- Remember to be careful when using bleach; wear old clothes and keep household items out of reach in case of a spill.

10

MAGGIE CRAWFORD

• *Bleach It Out*

MATERIALS

Rubber Stamps: Flower Vase by A Stamp In The Hand; Earth Laughs by Annette Watkins for PrintWorks Collection

Papers: Black and Cream Cardstock

Colored Pencils: Red, Orange, Yellow, Green and Blue

Adhesives: Glue Stick

Other: Undiluted Bleach

Tools: Blend and Flo Pen by Dove Brushes; Embossing Heat Tool; Paper Cutter

INSTRUCTIONS

1. Fill Blend and Flo Pen with freshly opened, undiluted bleach.
2. Paint bleach on stamps and press onto black cardstock.
3. Apply heat to image until bleach dries and brightens.
4. Use colored pencils when image is dry.
5. Cut and mat artwork onto cream cardstock; adhere to folded black card.

Note: For a simpler version of this card omit step four and leave image uncolored.

TIPS

• Use a small amount of bleach; overdoing it will smudge the stamped image.
• Another option for applying bleach directly to a rubber stamp is using a bleach-soaked sponge placed in a saucer. Stamp onto sponge as you would an inkpad.
• Experiment with a variety of paper types to see different results in color change.

TIPS

• There are several methods for inking cardstock freehand. ColorBox PetalPoints and Queues work well because each colored pad is removable. Ink can be brushed across the surface, dabbed or rubbed depending on desired look.

TIPS

• The embossed circle must be warm to take the stamp. If cooling occurs, reheat with heat tool and stamp again.

• A shoebox works great for embossing items that are too small to hold safely.

Dragonflies
JILL HAGLUND

MATERIALS

Rubber Stamps: Dragonfly and Small Leaf by A Stamp In The Hand; Leaf by Inkadinkado; Tulip Border by A Stamp In The Hand

Pigment Inkpads: ColorBox MetalExtra (Goldrush), ColorBox PetalPoint (Provence) and Top Boss Embossing (Clear) by Clearsnap

Dye Inkpads: Adirondack (Lettuce, Butterscotch and Pitch Black) by Ranger

Embossing Powders: Clear

Papers: Red, Textured Light Green, Dark Green, Black and Glossy White Cardstock; Black Mulberry Paper

Embellishments: Skeleton Leaf

Adhesives: Glue Stick; Tacky Glue

Other: Undiluted Bleach

Tools: Blend and Flo Pen by Dove Brushes; Embossing Heat Tool; Rubber Brayer; Scissors; Paper Cutter

TECHNIQUES
- Bleach It Out • Basic Resist
- Direct-to-Paper with Ink

INSTRUCTIONS

1. Cut and fold black cardstock and stamp Tulip Border in Goldrush, covering entire card; set ink with heat tool.
2. Tear black mulberry paper and adhere to card.
3. Use Bleach It Out technique (page 11) for Dragonfly and Leaf images. Stamp Leaf onto dark green cardstock and trim to size. Press Dragonfly onto red cardstock and tear edge for textured look. Set both aside.
4. Use Basic Resist technique (page 16) for background panel. Stamp Dragonfly in Clear several times over a panel of glossy white cardstock, layering the stamped images. Brayer Lettuce and Butterscotch dye inks on top.
5. Stamp Small Leaf in Clear onto red cardstock and apply embossing powder. Emboss image with heat tool and trim to size.
6. Cover textured light green cardstock with various shades from the PetalPoint; stamp Dragonfly in Pitch Black and cut out image.
7. Layer panel, dragonfly artwork and other embellishments over mulberry paper and adhere.

Falling Leaves
JILL HAGLUND

MATERIALS

Rubber Stamps: Leaf by Inkadinkado; Flower Icon by CC Rubber Stamps; Salal Branch by Fred Mullett; Floating Leaf by Hero Arts

Pigment Inkpads: ColorBox MetalExtra (Goldrush), ColorBox PetalPoint (Provence) and Top Boss Embossing (Clear) by Clearsnap

Dye Inkpads: Adirondack (Pitch Black) by Ranger

Embossing Powders: Gold, Green and Blue; Ultra Thick (Clear)

Papers: Textured Light Green, Dark Green, Black and Metallic Gold Cardstock; Specialty Paper

Embellishments: Chipboard

Adhesives: Glue Stick; Tacky Glue

Other: Undiluted Bleach; Spray Varnish; Small Bowl; Shoebox

Tools: X-ACTO™ Knife; Cutting Mat; Blend and Flo Pen by Dove Brushes; Embossing Heat Tool; Scissors; Paper Cutter

TECHNIQUES
- *Bleach It Out*
- *Ultra Thick Embossing*
- *Direct-to-Paper with Ink*

INSTRUCTIONS

1. Use Bleach It Out technique (pg 11) for Leaf image. Stamp Leaf onto dark green cardstock and trim to size; set aside.
2. Cover textured light green cardstock with various shades from the PetalPoint.
3. Stamp Salal Branch and Floating Leaf in Pitch Black over inked cardstock.
4. Cut and layer specialty paper, gold cardstock and inked cardstock as shown.
5. Using X-ACTO™ knife and cutting mat, cut a small circle out of chipboard to create a base.
6. Combine a small amount of each embossing powder in a bowl, creating a custom colored mixture.
7. Cover top and sides of circle with Clear embossing ink and apply powder mixture.
8. Place circle in shoebox and emboss with heat tool.
9. Stamp Flower Icon in Goldrush over embossed circle while warm, holding in place for 15 seconds. Lift stamp to complete the impression.
10. Seal the embossed circle with spray varnish and adhere to card along with bleached leaf.

Note: Specialty papers come in large sheets and can be found in fine art and craft stores.

Flower Mosaic
MAGGIE CRAWFORD

MATERIALS

Rubber Stamps: Flower by Penny Black; Definitions by Hero Arts; Splatter by Diana Kovacs for Hampton Art; Butterfly Wing (unknown)

Pigment Inkpads: ColorBox PetalPoint (Arboretum) by Clearsnap

Dye Inkpads: Adirondack (Butterscotch and Caramel) and Ancient Page (Azalea) by Ranger

Papers: Textured Purple, Lavender and Green Cardstock; White Cardstock

Markers/Pens: Green Brush Marker

Embellishments: Green Gingham Ribbon

Adhesives: Glue Stick; Tacky Glue

Tools: Stipple Brushes; Scissors; Paper Cutter

TECHNIQUES
• *Stipple Art* • *Blending Inks* • *Mosaic Art*

INSTRUCTIONS

1. Stipple white cardstock with purple and yellow shades from the PetalPoint, blending together.
2. Stamp Splatter in Butterscotch and Caramel on top of inked cardstock; stamp Definitions in Azalea.
3. Color stem of Flower stamp with green brush marker. Apply purple and orange shades from the PetalPoint to flower bud and stamp over inked cardstock.
4. Use similar colors from the PetalPoint on Butterfly Wing and stamp in upper corner; allow artwork to dry thoroughly.
5. Cut panel out of stamped cardstock; cut into eight equal pieces and mat onto textured green cardstock as shown.
6. Cut and mat textured lavender and purple cardstock onto folded green card.
7. Adhere green gingham ribbon and artwork panel in center.

TIPS
• Mosaic Art does not have to be in squares; experiment with this technique by cutting artwork into a variety of shapes before piecing back together.

Tri-fold Button Mosaic
MAGGIE CRAWFORD

MATERIALS

Stamps: Definitions by Hero Arts; Splatter by Diana Kovacs for Hampton Art; Butterfly Wing (unknown)

Pigment Inkpads: ColorBox PetalPoint (Arboretum) by Clearsnap

Dye Inkpads: Adirondack (Butterscotch and Caramel) and Ancient Page (Azalea) by Ranger

Papers: Textured Purple, Lavender and Gold Cardstock; White Cardstock

Embellishments: Purple Craft Thread; Purple Buttons

Adhesives: Glue Stick; Glue Dots by Glue Dots International

Tools: Stipple Brushes; Upholstery Needle; Scissors; Paper Cutter

TECHNIQUES
• *Stipple Art* • *Blending Inks* • *Mosaic Art*

INSTRUCTIONS

1. Stipple white cardstock with purple and yellow shades from the PetalPoint, blending together.
2. Stamp Splatter in Butterscotch and Caramel on top of inked cardstock; stamp Definitions in Azalea.
3. Apply various shades from the PetalPoint to Butterfly Wing and press lightly onto inked cardstock in several areas.
4. Trim panel out of stamped cardstock and cut into six equal pieces. Mat onto textured lavender and gold cardstock as shown.
5. Cut textured purple cardstock and fold opposite sides equally into center, creating tri-fold card.
6. Adhere artwork panels to card in random order.
7. Use upholstery needle to thread through button eyes several times for sewn appearance. Tie off thread in back.
8. Adhere "sewn" buttons to center of card with Glue Dots.
9. Cut 6" piece of thread and wrap around buttons diagonally to secure tri-fold.

Note: Gold Charm Mosaic by Maggie Crawford is made using the same techniques with gold charms added for embellishment.

Cherries

MAGGIE CRAWFORD

TECHNIQUES
- *Stipple Art* • *Basic Resist*
- *Stamping in Marker onto Glossy Paper*

MATERIALS

Rubber Stamps: Cherries by A Stamp In The Hand; Swirl Background by JudiKins

Pigment Inkpads: ColorBox MetalExtra (Goldrush) by Clearsnap

Dye Inkpads: Kaleidacolor Raised Rainbow (Desert Heat) by Tsukineko

Papers: Red, Dark Green and Glossy White Cardstock

Markers/Pens: Red and Green Brush Markers

Adhesives: Glue Stick

Tools: Stipple Brushes; Rubber Brayer; Embossing Heat Tool; Paper Cutter

INSTRUCTIONS

1. Stamp Swirl Background in Goldrush, covering white cardstock.
2. Brayer over images using dye ink.
3. Color Cherries with red and green brush markers and stamp over background; set ink with heat tool.
4. Stipple area around images with pink and orange shades from the Kaleidacolor until you achieve thorough coverage.
5. Cut and mat artwork onto dark green cardstock; adhere to folded red card.

TIPS
- In this technique, pigment ink resists dye ink and allows the original image to show through– it will only work on glossy cardstock.
- Provide several minutes of drying time (or use heat tool) between steps to avoid smearing.

Three Flowers

MAGGIE CRAWFORD

TECHNIQUE
- *Kaleidoscope Resist*

MATERIALS

Rubber Stamps: Flower by Penny Black; Dream by Dawn Houser for Inkadinkado

Pigment Inkpads: VersaMark Watermark (Clear) by Tsukineko

Dye Inkpads: Kaleidacolor Raised Rainbow (Flannel) by Tsukineko

Papers: Orange and Glossy White Cardstock

Adhesives: Glue Stick

Tools: Mesh Brayer by Fiskars; Rubber Brayer; Embossing Heat Tool; Paper Cutter

INSTRUCTIONS

1. Cover mesh brayer with Clear ink and run once over white cardstock.
2. Stamp Flower in Clear three times over mesh.
3. Roll brayer Flannel ink over images several times, always in the same direction.
4. Stamp Dream in a dark shade from the Kaleidacolor around Flower images; set ink with heat tool.
5. Cut and mat artwork onto folded orange card.

Note: Tulip Card by Maggie Crawford is made using the Kaleidoscope Resist technique.

TIPS
- VersaMark ink will resist dye ink in this project so don't be afraid to apply a lot of color.

TIPS

- Always bake clay in a well-ventilated room. Tools and equipment that come into contact with raw polymer clay should never be used to prepare food afterwards (including the oven); it is best to reserve sculpting tools and a toaster oven for clay-baking only.

Beaded Dragonfly Pin

JILL HAGLUND

MATERIALS

Rubber Stamps: Dragonfly by A Stamp In The Hand; Italian Poetry by Hero Arts

Pigment Inkpads: ColorBox MetalExtra (Goldrush) by Clearsnap

Dye Inkpads: Adirondack (Pitch Black) by Ranger

Embossing Powders: Gold

Papers: Textured Purple and Black Cardstock; White Cardstock; Specialty Paper

Embellishments: Black Wire; Leaf Bead

Adhesives: Glue Stick; E-6000 by Eclectic Products

Other: Purple Polymer Clay; Rub 'n Buff Wax Metallic Finish (Gold) by American Art Clay Company; Spray Varnish; Jewelry Pin Back; Paper Towel

Tools: X-ACTO™ Knife; Cutting Mat; Rolling Pin; Metal Spatula; Toothpick; Embossing Heat Tool; Toaster Oven; Paper Cutter

TECHNIQUE
• *Stamping in Polymer Clay*

INSTRUCTIONS

1. Stamp Italian Poetry in Pitch Black onto folded white card.
2. Stamp Italian Poetry in Goldrush onto textured black cardstock; apply embossing powder and emboss with heat tool.
3. Cut and tear embossed black paper, textured purple paper and specialty paper. Layer and adhere papers to folded white card and set aside.
4. Set toaster oven to 275° F.
5. Soften clay in hands and flatten with rolling pin on flat surface, (about 1/8" thickness).
6. Using a clean and dry stamp, press Dragonfly into clay.
7. Use X-ACTO™ knife over cutting mat to cut out impression and smooth edges with fingers. Pierce two holes on top of head with toothpick.
8. Bake in toaster oven for about 20 minutes. Remove with metal spatula and allow cooling time.
9. Rub clay dragonfly with metallic finish using a paper towel. This step will bring out details in the stamped image.
10. Cut wire into small pieces and glue in holes with strong adhesive to make antenna. Curl wire at tips by wrapping around toothpick.
11. Attach leaf bead and jewelry pin back with strong adhesive.
12. Once completed, seal clay pin with spray varnish and let dry.
13. Attach Dragonfly Pin to card by piercing top piece of paper and secure in place.

Dragonfly Panel

JILL HAGLUND

MATERIALS

Rubber Stamps: Dragonfly by Sarasota Stamps

Pigment Inkpads: ColorBox MetalExtra (Goldrush) and Top Boss Embossing (Clear) by Clearsnap

Embossing Powders: Green and Gold; Ultra Thick (Clear)

Papers: Black, White and Metallic Gold Cardstock; Gold Corrugated Cardboard; Specialty Paper

Embellishments: Chipboard

Adhesives: Glue Stick; Tacky Glue

Other: Spray Varnish; Small Bowl; Shoebox

Tools: X-ACTO™ Knife; Cutting Mat; Embossing Heat Tool; Paper Cutter

TECHNIQUE
• *Ultra Thick Embossing*

INSTRUCTIONS

1. Using X-ACTO™ knife and cutting mat, cut panel of chipboard to create base.
2. Follow the Ultra Thick Embossing technique (pg 13) to create Dragonfly Panel.
3. Stamp Dragonfly in Goldrush on embossed panel while warm. Hold in place for 15 seconds and lift to complete the impression.
4. Apply spray varnish to panel to seal pigment ink.
5. Mat panel onto black and gold cardstock, gold corrugated cardboard and specialty paper as shown; adhere to folded white card.

TIPS Instead of buying colored corrugated cardboard try creating your own. Save corrugated light bulb box inserts and color with spray paint.

Butterfly in Jar

JILL HAGLUND, ORIGINAL BY JOEY LONG

MATERIALS

Rubber Stamps: Jar by Dee Gruenig from Posh Impressions for Rubber Stampede; Butterfly by Personal Stamp Exchange; Dream by Acey Deucy; Dragonfly Circle and Insect Wings by Stampers Anonymous

Pigment Inkpads: ColorBox MetalExtra (Goldrush) and ColorBox PetalPoint (Mist and Aurora) and Top Boss Embossing (Clear) by Clearsnap

Dye Inkpads: Adirondack (Cobalt Blue) by Ranger

Embossing Powders: Gold; Ultra Thick (Clear)

Papers: White Cardstock

Colored Pencils: Pink, Yellow, Green, Blue and Purple Watercolor

Embellishments: White Tag; Purple Tulle; Gold Ribbon; Gold Thread; Beads

Adhesives: Tacky Glue; Adhesive Foam Tape

Other: Empty Plastic Produce Bags; Small Bowl of Water; Shoebox

Tools: Stipple Brushes; Embossing Heat Tool; Small Paintbrush; Scissors; Paper Cutter

TIPS
• Plastic produce bags make great craft tools. Cut bags in strips or squares and use as embellishments or stencils.

INSTRUCTIONS

1. Cut strips from empty produce bags and lay over folded white card.
2. Ink over strips with purple and blue shades from the PetalPoint.
3. Remove strips and stipple white tag with blue shades from the PetalPoint. Stamp Dream in Cobalt Blue and adhere tag to card.
4. Stamp wing of Butterfly in Goldrush in corner of card. Apply gold embossing powder and emboss with heat tool.
5. Color embossed wing with watercolor pencils and lightly go over colors with wet paintbrush.
6. Attach purple tulle to card with tacky glue.
7. Stamp Jar in Goldrush onto plain white cardstock twice. Apply gold embossing powder to one image and emboss with heat tool.
8. Cut out embossed image and set aside. Cut out inside of jar on second image to use as a template.
9. Shade template with watercolor pencils and paint with water to bleed colors; allow drying time.
10. Lightly stamp Insect Wings and Butterfly Circle in Pitch Black along edge.
11. Stamp Butterfly in Goldrush and emboss in gold; color Butterfly similar to wing.
12. Rub Clear embossing ink over stamped template and cover with ultra thick powder.
13. Place template in shoebox and emboss with heat tool.
14. Adhere template to inside of original embossed Jar.
15. Tie gold ribbon around Jar; thread and attach beads to ribbon.
16. Adhere artwork to card with adhesive foam tape.

Aspen Leaf
AMY WELLENSTEIN

MATERIALS

Rubber Stamps: Italian Text by Rubber Baby Buggy Bumpers; Script by A Stamp In The Hand; Aspen Leaf by Rubber Stampede

Dye Inkpads: Adirondack (Sepia, Lettuce, Oregano and Pitch Black) by Ranger

Papers: Green, Black and Metallic Gold Cardstock; Watercolor Paper

Markers/Pens: Brown Water-Based Marker

Adhesives: Glue Stick; Tape

Tools: Post-It® Notes or Removable Tape; Embossing Heat Tool; Water Bottle; Paper Cutter

INSTRUCTIONS

1. Apply Sepia, Lettuce, and Oregano inks to Aspen Leaf stamp; highlight edges with brown marker.
2. Lightly spritz inked stamp with water and press onto watercolor paper. Dry image with heat tool.
3. Create Post-It® Note template and mask leaf image. Stamp Italian Text in Pitch Black and Script in Sepia around leaf image – this process is called over-stamping.
4. Cut and mat artwork onto black and gold cardstock.
5. Cut a strip of black cardstock and wrap around folded green card, taping ends together.
6. Adhere artwork onto black strip.

Floral Vellum
AMY WELLENSTEIN

MATERIALS

Rubber Stamps: Architectural Cube by Stampendous

Pigment Inkpads: Top Boss Embossing (Clear) by Clearsnap

Embossing Powders: Clear

Papers: Black Cardstock; Printed Vellum by Autumn Leaves; Printed Text by 7gypsies for Autumn Leaves

Paints: Light Green and Black Acrylic

Embellishments: Chipboard

Adhesives: Glue Stick; Tacky Glue

Tools: X-ACTO™ Knife; Cutting Mat; Ruler; Embossing Heat Tool; Washcloth; Paintbrush

INSTRUCTIONS

1. Cut a square of chipboard using X-ACTO™ knife and ruler over cutting mat.
2. Paint chipboard with black acrylic and let dry.
3. Stamp Architectural Cube in Clear onto painted chipboard and apply embossing powder. Emboss image with heat tool.
4. Paint over embossed image with light green and allow drying time.
5. Use damp washcloth to scrub over surface of image until paint is removed.
6. Mat chipboard onto black cardstock with tacky glue.
7. Adhere Printed Vellum over Text paper with glue stick. Cut and mat layered papers to folded black card.
8. Attach embossed panel to card.

Scripted Leaf
AMY WELLENSTEIN

MATERIALS

Rubber Stamps: Scripted Leaf by Christine Adolph for Stampington & Co.

Dye Inkpads: Adirondack (Lettuce, Oregano, and Pitch Black) by Ranger

Papers: Green, Black and Cream Cardstock

Adhesives: Glue Stick

Tools: Paper Cutter

INSTRUCTIONS

1. Apply Lettuce ink to Scripted Leaf, covering entire stamp.
2. Dab Oregano ink on tips of leaves and Pitch Black on text.
3. Press stamp onto cream cardstock.
4. Cut and mat artwork onto black cardstock; adhere to folded green card.

TIPS
• To create a template, stamp onto Post-It® Note along adhesive edge and cut out image.

TIPS
• Don't be afraid to use several colors on one stamp. Start with lighter colors first to avoid staining your inkpads.

Purple Pears
MAGGIE CRAWFORD

MATERIALS

Rubber Stamps: Pear (Image) by Hampton Art; Pears (Word) by A Stamp In The Hand; Leaf by Stampington & Co.; Crackle by Stampers Anonymous; Large Shadow by Hero Arts

Pigment Inkpads: ColorBox Cat's Eye (Teal and Blue) by Clearsnap

Dye Inkpads: StâzOn (Royal Purple and Azure) by Tsukineko

Papers: Teal and White Cardstock

Adhesives: Glue Stick

Tools: Paper Cutter

TECHNIQUE
• *Transfer Shadow Stamping*

INSTRUCTIONS

1. Cover Large Shadow with Teal and Blue pigment inks. Work from top to bottom, light to dark, blending the colors together.
2. Ink Pear (image) in Royal Purple and press directly onto shadow stamp, over pigment ink.
3. Stamp around the edges with Leaf in Royal Purple.
4. Apply Azure to Crackle stamp and press over entire image.
5. Press shadow stamp firmly onto white cardstock.
6. Stamp Pears (word) in Royal Purple dye ink over transferred image.
7. Cut and mat artwork onto teal cardstock; adhere to folded white card.

TIPS
• Stamp dye inks carefully—the pigment-covered shadow stamp is slippery!
• Be aware that images will be reversed when they are stamped onto cardstock; add text after the transfer.

Green Teasel
MAGGIE CRAWFORD

MATERIALS

Rubber Stamps: Teasel by Fred Mullett; Butterfly by Magenta; Imagine, Explore and Discover by A Muse Artstamps; Crackle by Stampers Anonymous; Large Shadow by Hero Arts

Pigment Inkpads: ColorBox Cat's Eye (Yellow and Green) by Clearsnap

Dye Inkpads: StâzOn (Forest Green) by Tsukineko

Papers: Green and White Cardstock

Adhesives: Glue Stick

Tools: Paper Cutter

TECHNIQUE
• *Transfer Shadow Stamping*

INSTRUCTIONS

1. Cover Large Shadow with Yellow and Green pigment inks, blending together.
2. Ink Teasel in Forest Green and press directly onto shadow stamp.
3. Stamp around edges with Butterfly and Crackle stamps in Forest Green.
4. Press shadow stamp firmly onto white cardstock.
5. Stamp words in dye ink over transferred image.
6. Cut and mat artwork onto green cardstock; adhere to folded white card.

Note: Ferns and Flowers Card by Maggie Crawford is made using the Transfer Shadow Stamping technique. Stamps include: Flower and Dots by Magenta; Leaf by Stampington & Co.; Words by A Muse Artstamps.

TIPS

• StâzOn is a solvent-based inkpad, designed especially for non-porous surfaces such as glass, metal and plastic. These inks leave crisp and clear images on paper as well.

Cherish yesterday
Live for today
Dream of tomorrow

Cherish yesterday
Live for today
Dream of tomorrow

A

R

T

TIPS

• When purchasing copper sheets remember that a higher gauge means a thinner sheet.

Single Copper Leaf

AMY WELLENSTEIN

MATERIALS

Rubber Stamps: Leaf by Stampin' Up!

Pigment Inkpads: Top Boss Embossing (Clear) by Clearsnap

Embossing Powders: Clear

Papers: Green and Black Cardstock; Map by 7gypsies for Autumn Leaves

Embellishments: Eyelets by Making Memories; Chipboard

Adhesives: Glue Stick; Tacky Glue

Other: Liver of Sulfur Solution by Rio Grande; Fine Grit Sandpaper; 40 Gauge Copper Sheet; Small Bowl; Paper Towel

Tools: X-ACTO™ Knife; Cutting Mat; Ruler; Embossing Heat Tool; Eyelet Setting Tool; 1/8" Hole Punch; Paper Cutter

TECHNIQUE
• Copper Stamping

INSTRUCTIONS

1. Sand surface of copper sheet.
2. Stamp Leaf in Clear and apply embossing powder. Emboss image with heat tool and allow cooling time.
3. Fill small bowl with Liver of Sulfur and dip copper sheet in liquid.
4. Remove sheet once area around image turns black and allow drying time.
5. Buff copper piece with paper towel.
6. Cut a rectangle of chipboard using X-ACTO™ knife and ruler over cutting mat.
7. Wrap copper sheet around chipboard, keeping the leaf image in center.
8. Cut and mat Map paper onto black and green cardstock; adhere to folded black card.
9. Punch holes in corners of copper tile and set eyelets.
10. Adhere copper tile to center of card with tacky glue.

Note: Liver of Sulfur is a potassium sulfide mixture, traditionally used to darken or 'antique' silver or copper. It can be purchased in a solid or liquid form at art supply stores.

Cherish, Live, Dream

WAYNE DIELEMAN

MATERIALS

Rubber Stamps: Daisy, "Cherish, Live, Dream", Zigzag Border, Definitions and Alphabet by Hero Arts

Dye Inkpads: Adirondack (Sepia and Cranberry) by Ranger; StâzOn (Jet Black) by Tsukineko

Papers: Patterned, Script and Text Papers by 7gypsies; Textured Brown and Cream Cardstock; Specialty Paper

Markers/Pens: Red, Orange, Green and Brown Water-Based Markers

Embellishments: Yarn and Fibers; Clear Button; Star Brads; Tag Stickers; Jar with Sand

Adhesives: Glue Stick; Adhesive Foam Tape

Other: Staples; White Thread

Tools: Needle; Embossing Heat Tool; Water Bottle; Stapler; Scissors; Paper Cutter

TECHNIQUES
• Faux Watercolor with Marker and Dye Ink
• Collage with Ephemera

INSTRUCTIONS

1. Cut and mat Patterned paper to folded brown card.
2. Tear pieces of Text, Script and specialty papers; adhere to card as shown.
3. Color Daisy stamp with markers, blending together.
4. Lightly spritz inked stamp with water and press onto textured cream cardstock. Repeat this process for second flower and use heat tool to dry images.
5. Stamp "Cherish, Live, Dream" in Sepia around flowers.
6. Cut and tear artwork along edges and adhere to specialty paper, creating front flap. Add Zigzag Border in Cranberry along top of panel.
7. Stamp Definitions in Jet Black onto clear button and sew in place.
8. Staple flap along edge of card as shown.
9. Wrap yarn and fibers around card and tie along fold.
10. Stamp tag stickers with Alphabet stamps in black ink; adhere with adhesive foam tape.
11. Insert star brads along bottom of card and sew small jar in place for embellishment.

"If I had a world of my own, everything would be nonsense. Nothing would be what it is because everything would be what it isn't. And contrary-wise, what it is it wouldn't be, and what it wouldn't be, it would. You see?"

~ Alice, Alice in Wonderland by Lewis Carroll

Recreate yourself As often As you see fit!

*D*o you sometimes feel an urge to be playful in your art? What freedom of expression this can be. Even simple projects can make us fret over tiny details, but what enjoyment is there in that? Your passion to create is supposed to be pleasant and rewarding.

So we had extra fun being whimsical... just because! No rules, and no little voices saying, "Is this okay?" This chapter is full of fanciful creations through which the artists freed themselves and inspire you to do the same.

Whimsical Roosters
JILL HAGLUND

MATERIALS

Rubber Stamps: Roosters by Picture Show; Chicken Wire by JudiKins; Recreate Yourself by Kristen Powers for Stampotique Originals; Feather by Personal Stamp Exchange; Small Shadow by Hero Arts; Chicken Feet (unknown)

Pigment Inkpads: Encore! Ultimate Metallic (Silver) by Tsukineko

Dye Inkpads: StâzOn (Jet Black, Azure and Royal Purple) by Tsukineko

Embossing Powders: Silver

Papers: Red, Gold and White Cardstock; Specialty Paper

Embellishments: Feather

Adhesives: Tacky Glue

Other: Post-It® Notes or Removable Tape

Tools: Embossing Heat Tool; Scissors; Paper Cutter

TECHNIQUE
• *Paper Masking*

INSTRUCTIONS

1. Stamp Chicken Wire in Silver onto folded red card; apply embossing powder and emboss with heat tool.
2. Stamp Roosters in Jet Black onto white cardstock as shown.
3. Use the Paper Masking technique (pg 8) to hide first two images with Post-It® Notes.
4. Lightly over stamp all three Roosters with shadow stamp in Royal Purple.
5. Repeat this step using Azure ink on top of Royal Purple.
6. Remove paper masks and cut around images, creating panel.
7. Tear specialty paper and attach in center of card.
8. Adhere stamped panel to front of card and add feather for embellishment.
9. Cut gold cardstock to fit inside card and adhere additional torn specialty paper in center.
10. Stamp Recreate Yourself in Jet Black onto white cardstock.
11. Tear around image and adhere inside card over specialty paper.
12. Stamp Feather and Chicken Feet in black ink inside card as shown.

True Friend
KELLY LUNCEFORD

MATERIALS

Rubber Stamps: Alphabet by Personal Stamp Exchange

Dye Inkpads: Adirondack (Sepia) by Ranger

Papers: Green Cardstock; Floral and Striped Patterned Papers by K&Company

Embellishments: Brown Gingham and Green Ribbons; Silk Flower; Postage Stamp; Definition and Cherish Stickers by Making Memories; Clock Hands and Alphabet Stickers by Rebecca Sower for Nostalgiques for Stampington & Co.; Pin by 7gypsies

Adhesives: Glue Stick; Adhesive Foam Tape

Other: Gold Thread

Tools: Sewing Machine; Rectangle Punch by Marvy; Scissors; Paper Cutter

TECHNIQUE
• *Collage with Ephemera*

INSTRUCTIONS

1. Cut panel of Floral Patterned paper to fit front of folded green card.
2. Color edges of panel with Sepia ink for distressed look.
3. Adhere panel to card and distress edge of card in Sepia ink.
4. Sew zigzag pattern along bottom of card using sewing machine and gold thread.
5. Cut small panel from green cardstock and punch out center with rectangle punch, creating frame.
6. Tie green and brown gingham ribbons around frame, knotting pin in place as shown, and trim ends of ribbon.
7. Distress edges of frame in Sepia ink and stamp "friend" in Sepia using Alphabet stamps.
8. Mat frame onto Striped Patterned paper with adhesive foam tape and adhere to card.
9. Attach stickers, postage stamp and silk flower for embellishment.

Cherish
KELLY LUNCEFORD

MATERIALS

Dye Inkpads: StâzOn (Jet Black) by Tsukineko

Papers: Textured Red and Gold Cardstock; Paisley and Floral Patterned Papers by Daisy D's Paper Co.

Embellishments: Definition Sticker by Making Memories; Measuring Tape and Key Stickers by Rebecca Sower for Nostalgiques for Stampington & Co.; Assorted Ribbons; Black Photo Corners; Antique Button

Adhesives: Glue Stick; Tacky Glue

Tools: Scissors; Paper Cutter

TECHNIQUE
• *Collage with Ephemera*

INSTRUCTIONS

1. Cut panels of paisley Patterned Paper and gold cardstock to fit front of folded red card.
2. Wrap assorted ribbons around gold cardstock and tie in front.
3. Attach photo corners to one end of each panel.
4. Lay panels side-by-side and adhere.
5. Cut and mat Floral Patterned paper onto red cardstock.
6. Attach photo corners and adhere as shown.
7. Adhere stickers and antique button in place.
8. Color edge of card in Jet Black ink for distressed look.

Note: Yellow Dream card by Kelly Lunceford is made using the Collage with Ephemera technique.

TIPS
• Be certain to clean your paintbrush in between colors.

Prom Dress JILL HAGLUND

MATERIALS

Rubber Stamps: Dress by Dawn Houser for Inkadinkado; Hanger (unknown)

Pigment Inkpads: ColorBox MetalExtra (Goldrush) and ColorBox Pigment (Heliotrope) by Clearsnap

Embossing Powders: Gold

Papers: White and Embossed Yellow Cardstock; Watercolor Paper

Paints: Yellow, Green, Blue, Purple and Pink Watercolors

Markers/Pens: Yellow Brush Marker

Embellishments: Purple Photo Corners by Canson; Purple Tulle; Feather; Rosebud

Adhesives: Glue Stick; Tacky Glue

Other: Paper Towels

Tools: Embossing Heat Tool; Paintbrush; Water Bottle; Scissors; Paper Cutter

TECHNIQUE

• *Stamping Over Watercolor*

INSTRUCTIONS

1. Spray watercolor paper with water bottle, fully saturating.
2. Blot excess water with paper towels.
3. Spray watercolor paints to moisten and paint colors onto paper as shown, blending together.
4. Allow artwork to dry overnight or dry with heat tool.
5. Stamp Dress in Goldrush over painted paper; apply embossing powder and emboss with heat tool.
6. Cut out image and set aside.
7. Stamp Hanger in Heliotrope over folded white card.
8. Trim embossed yellow paper to size and attach purple photo corners; adhere to card.
9. Color edges of card with yellow brush marker.
10. Layer tulle and feathers behind dress image and adhere in center of card.
11. Attach rosebud with tacky glue.

If the Shoe fits
JILL HAGLUND

MATERIALS

Rubber Stamps: Shoe by Rubbermoon Stamp Company; Large Swirl (unknown); Small Swirl by A Stamp in the Hand

Pigment Inkpads: ColorBox PetalPoint (Primary) by Clearsnap

Dye Inkpads: Adirondack (Raspberry) by Ranger

Papers: Pink, White, Metallic Silver and Gold Cardstock; Pink Corrugated Paper; White Iridescent Paper; Specialty Paper

Embellishments: Wide Gold Metallic Ribbon; Feathers; Sequins; Clear Beads; Speckled Tulle

Adhesives: Glue Stick; Tacky Glue

Other: Radiant Pearls by LuminArte

Tools: Embossing Heat Tool; Paint Brush; Scissors; Paper Cutter

TECHNIQUE
• *Radiant Pearls*

INSTRUCTIONS

1. Stamp Large Swirl and Small Swirl in variety of shades from the PetalPoint over pink cardstock.
2. Cut and mat onto white iridescent paper, pink corrugated paper and metallic gold cardstock; adhere to folded white card.
3. Use dry paintbrush to color white cardstock with pink and blue radiant pearls, blending colors together.
4. Stamp Shoe in Raspberry over colored cardstock.
5. Cut and mat image onto metallic silver cardstock.
6. Tear specialty paper and layer over wide gold ribbon and tulle; adhere to card.
7. Adhere sequins, beads and feathers as shown.
8. Attach stamped panel in center of card.

TIPS

• Radiant Pearls are a water-soluble medium applied with a paintbrush. This product is easy to blend and glides over papers nicely, leaving a translucent finish. Water may be applied after radiant pearls are on paper for a different look, however much of the shimmer is lost.

Little Butterfly Girl
RENEE PLAINS

TECHNIQUE
- *Collage with Stamps*

INSTRUCTIONS

Rubber Stamps: Ace by Paperbag Studios; Ruler by Stampotique Originals; XOXO by Rubbermoon Stamp Company

Pigment Inkpads: VersaMagic Chalk Ink (Cloud White) by Tsukineko

Dye Inkpads: Adirondack (Espresso) by Ranger

Papers: Blue and Ivory Cardstock; Blue Gingham Paper; Button Patterned Paper; Floral Patterned Paper

Pastels/Chalks: Pink and Flesh Toned Chalks

Markers/Pens: Black and White Markers

Embellishments: Hook and Eye Card; Butterfly Wings

Adhesives: Glue Stick; Adhesive Foam Tape

Tools: Cotton Swabs; Scissors; Paper Cutter

MATERIALS

1. Stamp Ruler in Cloud White along top of folded blue card.
2. Attach hook and eye card with adhesive foam tape.
3. Stamp Ace in Espresso onto ivory cardstock; color image with chalks as shown and cut out face.
4. Create dress out of floral and button patterned papers and triangle hat out of blue gingham paper.
5. Piece together doll, attaching butterfly wings in back and adhere doll to card.
6. Draw legs and feet with markers as shown.
7. Stamp XOXO in Cloud White along bottom of card.

Butterfly Girl
AMY WELLENSTEIN

TECHNIQUE
- *Collage with Stamps*

INSTRUCTIONS

Rubber Stamps: Butterfly Girl by Claudine Hellmuth; Antique Border by Stampotique Originals

Dye Inkpads: Adirondack (Espresso) by Ranger

Papers: Brown and White Cardstock; Alpha Pistachio by BasicGrey; Black Text Paper

Pastels/Chalks: Blue, Purple, Pink and Flesh Toned Chalks

Embellishments: Ticket Stub; Heart Tag

Adhesives: Glue Stick; Tacky Glue

Tools: Cotton Swabs; Scissors; Paper Cutter

MATERIALS

1. Stamp Butterfly Girl in Espresso onto white cardstock.
2. Highlight with chalks using cotton swabs and cut out image.
3. Trim Alpha Pistachio paper to size and adhere Butterfly Girl in center.
4. Attach panel to folded brown card.
5. Stamp Antique Border in Espresso along top of card.
6. Cut small crown from black text paper.
7. Add crown, heart tag and ticket stub for embellishment.

TIPS • Try creating postcards on sturdy corrugated cardboard for a unique look.

Happy Birthday Girl
CAROLYN PEELER

MATERIALS

Rubber Stamps: Script by Stampers Anonymous; Alphabet by Hero Arts

Pigment Inkpads: Encore! Ultimate Metallic (Silver) by Tsukineko

Dye Inkpads: StâzOn (Jet Black) by Tsukineko; Tim Holtz Distress Ink (Tea Dye) and Adirondack (Espresso) by Ranger

Embossing Powders: Silver

Papers: White Cardstock; Polka Dot, Green Paisley, Green Striped and Script Papers by Melissa Frances

Embellishments: Vintage Photo; Silver Wire; Alphabet Beads; Silk Flower; White Buttons

Adhesives: Glue Stick; Tacky Glue; Glue Dots by Glue Dots International; Tape

Other: White Craft Thread

Tools: Upholstery Needle; Scissors; Paper Cutter

TECHNIQUE
• *Collage with Ephemera*

INSTRUCTIONS

1. Stamp Script in Espresso onto folded white card.
2. Edge card in Silver pigment ink; apply embossing powder and emboss with heat tool.
3. Trim Green Paisley and Striped papers and distress edges with Tea Dye ink; mat papers onto card as shown.
4. Cut around vintage photo, creating silhouette image.
5. Cut wings from Script paper and party hat from Polka Dot paper and adhere onto silhouette image.
6. Stamp phrase "happy" in Jet Black onto plain white cardstock; cut out phrase and adhere in place.
7. Trim small piece of white cardstock; distress edges in Tea Dye and mat along bottom of card.
8. Use upholstery needle to thread through button eyes several times for sewn appearance. Tie off thread in back.
9. Adhere "sewn" buttons to white cardstock with Glue Dots.
10. Use upholstery needle to create holes for wire placement. String silver wire with letter beads and insert ends through holes. Tape off wire ends inside card.
11. Attach additional "sewn" button in center of silk flower with Glue Dot and adhere to card as shown.
12. Sew zigzag pattern between Paisley panel and card.

Thank You
AMY WELLENSTEIN

MATERIALS

Rubber Stamps: Alphabet by Stampotique Originals

Dye Inkpads: StâzOn (Jet Black) by Tsukineko; Adirondack (Salmon and Peach Bellini) by Ranger

Papers: Glossy White Cardstock; Corrugated Cardboard

Embellishments: Silk Flower; Black Brads

Adhesives: Tacky Glue

Tools: 1/8" Hole Punch; Embossing Heat Tool; Stylus; Scissors; Paper Cutter

TECHNIQUE
• *Direct-to-Glossy Paper with Dye Ink*

INSTRUCTIONS

1. Trim panel of glossy white cardstock to size.
2. Lightly rub cardstock edges with Jet Black dye ink.
3. Use stylus to apply Salmon and Peach Bellini ink over cardstock; set ink with heat tool.
4. Stamp "Thank You" phrase in Jet Black using Alphabet stamps.
5. Cut and mat artwork onto corrugated cardstock.
6. Punch holes for brad placement and insert brads.
7. Adhere silk flower as shown.

Note: Birthday Wishes card by Carolyn Peeler is made using the Collage with Ephemera technique. Rubber stamps by Hero Arts, papers by Melissa Frances.

TIPS
• Be sure to allow drying time between steps when stamping on glossy cardstock to avoid fingerprints and smears; expedite this process by using a heat tool.

Java Post
JILL HAGLUND

MATERIALS

Rubber Stamps: Java Post, Coffee Phrase and Postage by Rubberstamp Ave.; Coffee Cup and Coffee Bean Border by Ann-ticipations; Coffee Blockbuster by Embossing Arts Co.; Numbers by Hero Arts; Triangle Post (unknown)

Dye Inkpads: StâzOn (Jet Black and Timber Brown) by Tsukineko; Adirondack (Ginger, Rust, Sepia and Meadow) by Ranger

Papers: Pre-Folded Corrugated Cardboard; Brown, White and Glossy White Cardstock

Markers/Pens: Black Fine-Tip Pen

Adhesives: Glue Stick; Tacky Glue

Other: Post-It® Notes or Removable Tape

Tools: Stipple Brush; Decorative Scissors; Scissors; Paper Cutter

TECHNIQUES
• *Stipple Art* • *Paper Masking*
• *Postage Stamping*

INSTRUCTIONS

1. Stipple over entire panel of white cardstock in Timber Brown and stipple edges in Meadow.
2. Stamp collage of images in Timber Brown over stippled cardstock. Stamp Java Post in black ink.
3. Cut and mat artwork onto brown cardstock; adhere to pre-folded corrugated cardboard.
4. Stamp various postage stamps in Jet Black onto glossy white cardstock.
5. Use the Paper Masking technique (pg 8) to hide borders of postage stamps with Post-It® Notes.
6. Stipple inside postage stamps in various brown shades by Adirondack.
7. Over stamp collage of images in Rust and Ginger, and stamp Coffee Phrase in Jet Black.
8. Remove masks and cut out individual posts with either straight or decorative-edged scissors; adhere to card.
9. Stamp Numbers as shown and draw in symbol for cent sign.

Must Have Coffee!
JILL HAGLUND

MATERIALS

Rubber Stamps: Cappuccino Lady and Coffee Phrase by Rubberstamp Ave.; Coffee Bean by Ann-ticipations; Tea Cup (unknown)

Dye Inkpads: StâzOn (Jet Black) by Tsukineko; Adirondack (Ginger, Terra Cotta and Butterscotch) by Ranger

Papers: Pre-Folded Corrugated Cardboard; Gold Cardstock; Specialty Paper

Colored Pencils: Red, Blue, Pink and Flesh Toned

Embellishments: Large Tag; Burlap

Adhesives: Adhesive Foam Tape; Tacky Glue

Tools: Scissors; Paper Cutter

TECHNIQUE
• *Collage with Stamps*

INSTRUCTIONS

1. Cut off bottom half of large tag. Rub Butterscotch ink over top half, distressing edges.
2. Stamp Coffee Bean in Butterscotch and Coffee Phrase in Jet Black over inked tag and set aside.
3. Stamp Cappuccino Lady in Ginger onto gold cardstock.
4. Highlight with colored pencils and cut out image.
5. Stamp Tea Cup in Terra Cotta onto gold cardstock and cut out image.
6. Layer and adhere burlap piece, specialty paper and stamped artwork onto pre-folded corrugated cardboard as shown.

Note: Cup of Joe card by Jill Haglund is made using the Collage with Stamps technique. Large coffee cup by Post Script Studio, Coffee Background by Rubberstamp Avenue.

Renee's Doll
RENEE PLAINS

MATERIALS

Rubber Stamps: Doll by Rubbermoon Stamp Company; Tapa Block by Stampendous; Alphabet and Numbers by Stamp Out Cute; Buttons by Nina Bagley

Dye Inkpads: Adirondack (Winter Sky and Ginger) and Archival Ink (Coffee) by Ranger

Papers: Ivory Cardstock; Script Paper by 7gypsies

Pastels/Chalks: Tan and Pink Chalk

Embellishments: Jewelry Tags

Adhesives: Glue Stick; Adhesive Foam Tape

Tools: Cotton Swabs; Scissors; Paper Cutter

INSTRUCTIONS

1. Stamp Doll in Ginger onto ivory cardstock.
2. Highlight cheeks with pink chalk using cotton swabs.
3. Cut out image creating doll silhouette and set aside.
4. Stamp Tapa Block in Winter Sky several times onto ivory cardstock.
5. Create skirt out of stamped cardstock and attach to doll image.
6. Cut and mat Script paper onto folded ivory card.
7. Adhere doll to card, folding arms up for dimension.
8. Stamp Buttons in Coffee onto ivory cardstock; cut out image and adhere along top of card.
9. Stamp Alphabet and Numbers in Coffee ink onto jewelry tags as shown.
10. Lightly color tags with tan chalk for aged appearance.
11. Add tags to card for embellishment, adhering string under doll's hand.
12. Create dimension by adhering "Doll" tag with adhesive foam tape.

Follow Your Dreams
ROBEN-MARIE SMITH

TECHNIQUES
- *Direct-to-Paper with Chalk Ink*
- *Highlight Coloring with Watercolor Pencils*

MATERIALS

Rubber Stamps: Spelling, Buttons and Ace by Paperbag Studios

Pigment Inkpads: ColorBox Queue Chalk Ink (Chocolates and Blueberries) by Clearsnap

Dye Inkpads: StâzOn (Jet Black) by Tsukineko

Papers: Plaid Striped Paper by K&Company; French Text

Colored Pencils: Yellow, Blue, Brown and Flesh Toned Watercolor

Embellishments: Rub-on Words and Black Mini Brads by Making Memories

Adhesives: Glue Stick

Other: Small Bowl of Water

Tools: 1/8" Hole Punch; Small Paintbrush; Scissors; Paper Cutter

INSTRUCTIONS

1. Use a blue shade from the Queue Chalk Ink and rub onto dark blue cardstock.
2. Stamp Buttons and Spelling in black ink onto chalked panel and allow drying time.
3. Cut and mat artwork onto Plaid Striped paper; adhere to folded blue card.
4. Tear French text around edge and adhere in center. Punch holes for brad placement and insert brads.
5. Stamp Ace in black ink onto white cardstock and color with watercolor pencils. Lightly go over colors with wet paintbrush to blend.
6. Cut and mat artwork onto Plaid Striped paper and adhere to card. Add rub-on words for embellishment.

TIPS
- Be sure to rub the chalk inkpad gently to avoid transferring the outline shape of the pad onto the paper.

Live Life
AMY WELLENSTEIN

TECHNIQUES
- *Paper Masking* • *Chalk Popping*
- *Coloring with Chalk*

MATERIALS

Rubber Stamps: Live Life by Paperbag Studios; Dots by Hot Potatoes

Pigment Inkpads: VersaMark Watermark (Clear) and VersaFine (Onyx Black) by Tsukineko

Papers: Red, Black and White Cardstock

Pastels/Chalks: Red, Green, Blue and Flesh Toned Chalks

Adhesives: Glue Stick

Other: Post-It® Notes; Removable Tape; Spray Fixative

Tools: Cotton balls; Cotton Swabs; Paper Cutter

INSTRUCTIONS

1. Stamp Live Life in Onyx Black onto white cardstock panel.
2. Use the Paper Masking technique (pg 8) to hide the image with Post-It® Notes. Mask edge of cardstock with removable tape to create border.
3. Over stamp Dots in Clear Watemark around masked image.
4. Allow ink to dry for two to three minutes.
5. Apply green and yellow chalks over background using cotton balls. Shake off excess chalk.
6. Remove mask from image and color with chalks using cotton swabs. Remove tape from edge to reveal white border.
7. Spray chalked paper with fixative and allow drying time.
8. Cut and mat artwork onto red cardstock; adhere to folded black card.

TIPS
- Try holding the cotton ball in place with a clothespin to avoid a mess or possibly getting fingerprints on your artwork.
- Fresh makeup applicators make great tools for applying chalks as well.

The term retro is used to describe objects and attitudes that no longer seem modern but have instead become old fashioned or timeless. With sweet reminiscence, we may be reminded of past times, cultures and trends.

Get ready to stroll down memory lane. The artwork portrayed in this chapter will transport you back in time while teaching you current techniques in the rubber stamping world such as chalk popping, collage with stamps and highlight coloring with watercolor pencils. So dig out your marigold yellows, olive greens and baby blues—in chalks, inks and pencils—for creative cards featuring some fabulous retro images.

"When I get home I shall write a book about this place...if I ever do get home."

~ Alice, Alice in Wonderland by Lewis Carroll

Olive Rose

AMY WELLENSTEIN

MATERIALS

Rubber Stamps: Angel Definition, Numeric, Alpha, Dots, Olive Rose and Spiraling Out of Control by Stampotique Originals

Pigment Inkpads: VersaMark Watermark (Clear), VersaMagic Chalk Ink (Cloud White) and VersaFine (Onyx Black) by Tsukineko

Dye Inkpads: Adirondack (Lettuce) by Ranger; Kaleidacolor Raised Rainbow (Spring Greens) by Tsukineko

Papers: Green, Black and White Cardstock

Pastels/Chalks: Yellow, Green, Pink and Flesh Toned Chalks

Markers/Pens: Silver Leafing Pen by Krylon

Adhesives: Glue Stick

Other: Post-It® Notes or Removable Tape; Spray Fixative

Tools: Cotton Balls; Cotton Swabs; Paper Cutter

TECHNIQUES
- *Paper Masking*
- *Chalk Popping*
- *Coloring with Chalks*

INSTRUCTIONS

1. Stamp Olive Rose in Onyx Black onto white cardstock.
2. Use the Paper Masking technique (pg 8) to hide image with Post-It® Notes.
3. Over stamp Dots in Clear Watermark around masked image.
4. Allow ink to dry for two to three minutes.
5. Apply green and yellow chalks over background using cotton balls. Shake off excess chalk.
6. With mask still in place, over stamp Angel Definition in Onyx Black, Numeric in Lettuce and Spiraling out of Control in a green shade from the Kaleidacolor.
7. Remove mask and color Olive Rose with chalks using cotton swabs.
8. Spray chalked paper with fixative and allow drying time.
9. Cut and mat artwork onto black cardstock and edge with silver leafing pen.
10. Stamp Spiraling out of Control in Cloud White onto plain black cardstock.
11. Cut and mat stamped cardstock to folded green card.
12. Adhere original artwork to card.
    Note: Olive Rose card is pictured on page 43.

Bathing Beauties

AMY WELLENSTEIN

MATERIALS

Rubber Stamps: Beauties and Sun by Stampotique Originals; Bangkok Post by Tin Can Mail; Postage Blank by Renaissance Art Stamps

Pigment Inkpads: VersaFine (Onyx Black) by Tsukineko

Papers: Teal, Black and White Cardstock; Patterned Paper by Chatterbox

Pastels/Chalks: Yellow, Green, Blue, Pink and Flesh Toned Chalks

Adhesives: Glue Stick

Other: Spray Fixative

Tools: Cotton Swabs; Scissors; Paper Cutter

TECHNIQUES
- *Coloring with Chalks*
- *Postage Stamping*

INSTRUCTIONS

1. Stamp Beauties and Sun in Onyx Black onto white cardstock.
2. Color images with chalks using cotton swabs and spray with fixative; set aside.
3. Stamp Postage Blank in Onyx Black onto plain white cardstock.
4. Cut chalk artwork into quadrants and adhere inside postage lines.
5. Stamp Bangkok Post in black ink on upper left and lower right corners.
6. Cut and mat artwork onto teal cardstock and Patterned paper; adhere to folded black card.

TIPS
- If you find cutting your artwork to size difficult, try stamping the Postage Blank over the chalk art and cutting inside the lines.

44

TIPS
- Instead of using a spray fixative you can place tissue paper over chalked artwork and rub over images with a bone folder to set chalk.
- For additional tips on chalk art go to plaidonline.com and search for chalk tips. This website has numerous ideas and step-by-step photos for various techniques.

Modern Woman

AMY WELLENSTEIN

MATERIALS

Rubber Stamps: Modern Woman by Stampotique Originals; Italian Text by Rubber Baby Buggy Bumpers

Pigment Inkpads: VersaFine (Onyx Black) by Tsukineko

Dye Inkpads: Adirondack (Rust) by Ranger

Papers: Red, Green, Black and White Cardstock

Pastels/Chalks: Pink, Orange, Yellow and Flesh Toned Chalks

Embellishments: Black Brads by Making Memories; Petite Tabs by 7gypsies

Adhesives: Glue Stick

Other: Post-It® Notes or Removable Tape; Spray Fixative

Tools: Cotton Ball; Cotton Swabs; Paper Cutter

TECHNIQUES
- *Paper Masking*
- *Coloring with Chalks*

INSTRUCTIONS

1. Stamp Modern Woman in Onyx Black onto white cardstock.
2. Use the Paper Masking technique (pg 8) to hide the image with Post-It® Notes.
3. Stamp Italian Text in Rust over masked image.
4. Apply yellow chalk over background using cotton ball. Shake off excess chalk.
5. Remove paper mask and use cotton swabs to color image as shown.
6. Spray chalk artwork with fixative and allow drying time.
7. Cut and mat onto black cardstock.
8. Attach panel to red cardstock using petite tabs and brads; adhere to folded green card.

Dream

ROBEN-MARIE SMITH

MATERIALS

Rubber Stamps: Live Life by Paperbag Studios

Dye Inkpads: StâzOn (Jet Black) by Tsukineko

Papers: Book Print by Li'l Davis Designs; Antique Barcode by KI Memories; Green Floral by Anna Griffin; Dark Green and White Cardstock

Pastels/Chalks: Green, Blue and Flesh Toned Chalks

Embellishments: Black Mini Brads, Pewter Frame and Rub-on Word by Making Memories; Butterfly Sticker by K&Company; Green Gingham Ribbon

Adhesives: Glue Stick; Tacky Glue

Other: Spray Fixative

Tools: 1/8" Hole Punch; Cotton Swabs; Paper Cutter

TECHNIQUES

- *Coloring with Chalks*
- *Collage with Ephemera*

INSTRUCTIONS

1. Cut and mat Antique Barcode paper to folded dark green card.
2. Trim and attach Book Print and Green Floral papers as shown; punch holes and attach mini brads on top and bottom.
3. Stamp Live Life in black ink onto white cardstock and color with chalks using cotton swabs. Spray with fixative and allow drying time.
4. Trim image to fit behind pewter frame.
5. Tie ribbon through holes of frame and adhere image inside. Attach to card with tacky glue.
6. Place butterfly sticker and rub-on word on card as shown.

   Note: Best Friend card by Robin-Marie Smith is made using the Coloring with Chalks technique with additional embellishments. All rubber stamps are by Paperbag Studios.

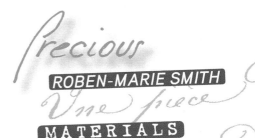

Precious

ROBEN-MARIE SMITH

MATERIALS

Rubber Stamps: Best Friends by Paperbag Studios

Pigment Inkpads: VersaFine (Onyx Black) by Tsukineko

Papers: Striped Paper by Making Memories; Patterned Paper by K&Company; Brown Coffee Paper by Pebbles; Paper Ephemera; White Cardstock

Embellishments: Precious Sticker by Bo-Bunny Press; Flower Sticker by K&Company; Black Mini Brads by Making Memories

Adhesives: Glue Stick

Tools: 1/8" Hole Punch; Paper Cutter

TECHNIQUE

• *Collage with Stamps*

INSTRUCTIONS

1. Stamp Best Friends in Onyx Black onto brown coffee paper. Cut around image and tear along bottom; set aside.

2. Cut and mat Striped paper to folded white card.

3. Tear script ephemera and layer behind Brown Coffee paper and Patterned paper; adhere to card.

4. Tear numerical ephemera into strip and adhere in center.

5. Place stamped image panel as shown.

6. Punch holes for brad placement and attach mini brads.

7. Adhere stickers in place.

Try 2 Be Different
AMY WELLENSTEIN

MATERIALS

Rubber Stamps: Beauties by Stampotique Originals; Beaded Background by JudiKins; Large Fuzzy Alphabet by Postmodern Design; Classic Alphabet by All Night Media/Plaid Enterprises

Pigment Inkpads: VersaMark Watermark (Clear) and VersaFine (Onyx Black) by Tsukineko

Papers: Black and White Cardstock; Red and Text Patterned Papers by 7gypsies

Pastels/Chalks: Red, Orange, Yellow, Green, Blue and Flesh Toned Chalks

Adhesives: Glue Stick

Other: Post-It® Notes or Removable Tape; Spray Fixative

Tools: Cotton Balls; Cotton Swabs; Scissors; Paper Cutter

TECHNIQUES
• *Paper Masking* • *Chalk Popping*
• *Coloring with Chalks*

INSTRUCTIONS

1. Stamp Beauties in Onyx Black onto white cardstock.
2. Use the Paper Masking technique (pg 8) to hide the image with Post-It® Notes.
3. Over stamp Beaded Background in Clear Watermark around image.
4. Allow ink to dry for two to three minutes.
5. Apply red, orange and yellow chalks to background with cotton balls. Shake off excess chalk.
6. Stamp phrase using various alphabet stamps in black ink over chalk artwork.
7. Remove paper mask and highlight image with chalks using cotton swabs. Spray artwork with fixative and allow drying time.
8. Hand-cut party hats out of Text Patterned paper and adhere as shown.
9. Cut and mat artwork onto black cardstock and Red Patterned paper; adhere to folded black card.

Sweetness
AMY WELLENSTEIN

MATERIALS

Rubber Stamps: Girl and Sweetness by Rubbermoon Stamp Company; Art Definition and Long Label by Stampotique Originals; Stars by Rubber Soul; Dots by Hot Potatoes

Pigment Inkpads: VersaMark Watermark (Clear) and VersaFine (Onyx Black) by Tsukineko

Dye Inkpads: Adirondack (Lettuce) by Ranger

Papers: Brown, Black and White Cardstock; Pistachio Paper by BasicGrey

Pastels/Chalks: Orange, Yellow, Pink and Flesh Toned Chalks

Adhesives: Glue Stick; Adhesive Foam Tape

Other: Post-It® Notes; Removable Tape; Spray Fixative

Tools: Cotton Balls; Cotton Swabs; Scissors; Paper Cutter

TECHNIQUES
• *Paper Masking* • *Chalk Popping* • *Coloring with Chalks*

INSTRUCTIONS

1. Stamp Girl in Onyx Black onto white cardstock.
2. Use the Paper Masking technique (pg 8) to create mask for girl silhouette.
3. Over stamp Art Definition in black ink.
4. Remove mask and color image with yellow and flesh toned chalks using cotton swabs; cut out and set aside.
5. Use the Paper Masking technique to create a border around plain white cardstock panel.
6. Inside border, stamp Stars in Clear Watermark and allow ink to dry for two to three minutes.
7. Apply orange and pink chalks over background with cotton balls. Shake off excess chalk.
8. Stamp Dots in Lettuce over star images.
9. Remove paper mask around border of cardstock and spray artwork with fixative.
10. Cut around chalk artwork leaving thin white border and mat onto black cardstock and Pistachio paper; adhere to folded brown card.
11. Adhere Girl image in center of card.
12. Stamp Long Label in black ink onto plain white cardstock and stamp Sweetness inside.
13. Cut out label and attach along bottom of card with adhesive foam tape.

Note: Family card by Amy Wellingstein is made using the Chalk Popping and Paper Masking techniques with additional embellishments. All rubber stamps are by Stampotique Originals.

friends
ROBEN-MARIE SMITH

MATERIALS

Rubber Stamps: Best Friends by Paperbag Studios; Alphabet and Numbers by Hero Arts

Dye Inkpads: StâzOn (Jet Black and Timber Brown) by Tsukineko

Papers: Brown Cardstock; Patterned Paper; French Text Ephemera

Colored Pencils: Brown

Embellishments: Brown Gingham and Gold Ribbon; Daisy Trim; Black Button; Silk Flower; Coffee-Dyed Tag; Metal Hardware

Adhesives: Glue Stick; Tacky Glue

Tools: Scissors; Paper Cutter

INSTRUCTIONS

1. Stamp Best Friends in Timber Brown and appropriate numbers in Jet Black onto coffee-dyed tag as shown.

2. Tear and adhere French text ephemera. Use brown colored pencil to circle "la laine" in French text.

3. Attach silk flower, button and brown gingham ribbon and adhere tag to center of folded brown card.

4. Trim and tear patterned and French text papers; layer and adhere along top of card. Stamp "friends" using Alphabet stamps in black ink over paper.

5. Tie gold ribbon through hardware and attach to corner of card.

6. Place daisy trim along bottom and adhere.

TECHNIQUES
- *Collage with Stamps*
- *Collage with Ephemera*

TIPS
- Old textbook pages make perfect ephemera for cards.
- Fabric trims add texture and dimension when used for embellishment.

Always Flowers
ROBEN-MARIE SMITH

MATERIALS

Rubber Stamps: There Are Always Flowers by Paperbag Studios; Paris Postage by Tin Can Mail; Old Writing by Hero Arts

Dye Inkpads: StâzOn (Jet Black) by Tsukineko

Papers: Secret Garden Solid by Daisy D's Paper Co.; Definition Paper by K&Company; School Days by Li'l Davis Designs; Brown and Black Cardstock

Embellishments: Large Embossed Vellum Flower by K&Company; Vintage Image from Collage Sheet by Paperbag Studios; Black Button

Adhesives: Glue Stick; Tacky Glue

Tools: Scissors; Paper Cutter

INSTRUCTIONS

1. Tear Secret Garden paper into strip and adhere in center of folded brown card. Cut and mat Definition paper on top and set aside.

2. Cut and mat School Days paper and Vintage Image onto black cardstock.

3. Stamp Paris Postage and Old Writing in black ink over panel; adhere to card.

4. Stamp There Are Always Flowers in black ink onto Secret Garden paper and cut out individual words; adhere along right side of card.

5. Cut out embossed vellum flower and adhere in place. Attach button to center of flower with tacky glue.

51

The "warm fuzzies" never feel as good as when they are wrapped up in a cozy blanket of nostalgia. A cup of hot tea with grandma, a stroll through her garden planted with loving care; it's comforting recollections like these that vintage artwork brings to mind.

This chapter includes vintage images and antique designs that will warm your heart and evoke those cherished memories. What a wonderful way to keep them alive, creating art that honors the special people no longer among us but that we will hold forever dear.

Delightful Child
ROBEN-MARIE SMITH

TECHNIQUES
- Dry Brush Painting
- Collage with Ephemera

MATERIALS

Rubber Stamps: First Grade by Paperbag Studios

Dye Inkpads: StâzOn (Jet Black) by Tsukineko

Papers: Fleur Rouge and Script Paper by 7gypsies; Black, White and Beige Cardstock

Paints: White Acrylic

Colored Pencils: Red

Embellishments: Safety Pins; Silk Flowers; Small Number Stencil; Definitions

Adhesives: Glue Stick; Tacky Glue

Tools: Label Maker; Paintbrush; Scissors; Paper Cutter

INSTRUCTIONS

1. Cut panel of beige cardstock and adhere small number stencil in place.
2. Use a dry paintbrush and lightly paint over panel and stencil with white acrylic.
3. Allow paint to dry thoroughly.
4. Mat panel onto folded black card.
5. Stamp First Grade in Jet Black onto white cardstock and highlight with red colored pencil.
6. Cut and mat image onto Fleur Rouge paper.
7. Trim Script paper into strips and adhere to card as shown.
8. Attach stamped panel in center of card.
9. Cut small piece of Fleur Rouge paper and tear in half.
10. Attach safety pins to torn paper and adhere to card.
11. Add silk flowers and definitions for embellishment.
12. Create "Peace" phrase with label make and adhere in place.

TIPS
- Dry brush painting creates a textured look on papers.

"The time has come, my little friends, to talk of other things. Of shoes and ships and sealing wax, of cabbages and kings. And why the sea is boiling hot, and whether pigs have wings.
~ Walrus, Alice in Wonderland by Lewis Carroll

Family of Three

JOEY LONG

MATERIALS

Rubber Stamps: Numbers by Wordsworth

Dye Inkpads: StâzOn (Jet Black) by Tsukineko

Papers: Black Cardstock; Book Text

Embellishments: Black Ribbon; Black Mini Brads by Making Memories; Vintage Image; Fibers

Adhesives: Glue Stick; Tacky Glue

Other: Beeswax

Tools: 1/8" Hole Punch; Label Maker; JudiKin's Color Duster; Mini Crock Pot; Scissors; Paper Cutter

INSTRUCTIONS

1. Cut and mat book text onto folded black card.
2. Stamp Numbers in Jet Black along side as shown.
3. Trim piece of black ribbon and attach along side of card.
4. Break off wax shavings and place them into mini crock pot.
5. Apply thin layer of wax over card using JudiKin's Color Duster.
6. Tear around vintage image and adhere in place with melted wax.
7. Punch holes for brad placement and insert black mini brads.
8. Use label maker to create phrase "family" and adhere.
9. Wrap fibers around fold of card and tie in front.

Note: Child with Flag card by Joey Long is made using the Encaustic Wax Art technique. Wooden Ruler Border by Postmodern Design and Altered Book Circle by Cat'slife Press.

TIPS

• Use caution when melting wax and keep crock pot on a medium to low temperature.

• Do not use candle wax or paraffin; these waxes are brittle and difficult to work with for collage purposes.

• Tools and equipment that come into contact with melted wax should not be used with food afterwards; reserve a crock pot for wax-melting only.

Leonardo Art
LOUISE KOLKER

MATERIALS

Rubber Stamps: Lace Border by Fancifuls, Inc.; Leonardo Art by Unicorn Stempel

Dye Inkpads: Adirondack (Cranberry and Bottle) by Ranger

Papers: Dark Green, Light Green and Textured Red Cardstock

Embellishments: Red Lace; Red Brads

Adhesives: Glue Stick; Tacky Glue

Tools: 1/8" Hole Punch; Scissors; Paper Cutter

INSTRUCTIONS

1. Stamp Leonardo Art in Bottle ink onto light green cardstock.
2. Cut image horizontally into three pieces, as shown, and mat onto dark green cardstock.
3. Punch holes along right side for brad placement and insert red brads.
4. Cut two panels of light green cardstock, one slightly larger than the other.
5. Stamp Lace Border in Cranberry along sides of smaller panel.
6. Punch holes in Lace Border image and cut along scalloped edge.
7. Adhere two pieces of red lace to sides of larger panel and cut around lace.
8. Cut and mat dark green cardstock onto folded red card.
9. Layer and adhere three panels as shown.

Photographs Hold the Key
LOUISE KOLKER

TECHNIQUE
- *Collage with Stamps*

MATERIALS

Rubber Stamps: Camera and Photographs Phrase by Lucy Stamps; Boys from Dream Notions Sheet by Paperbag Studios

Pigment Inkpads: VersaMagic Chalk Ink (Cloud White) and VersaFine (Onyx Black) by Tsukineko

Dye Inkpads: Archival Ink (Coffee) by Ranger

Papers: Red, Black and Cream Cardstock; Old Dictionary Text

Embellishments: Black Slide Die Cuts; Clip; Black Inspiration Tape by Club Scrap

Adhesives: Glue Stick; Glue Dots by Glue Dots International

Tools: Embossing Heat Tool; Die Cut Squeeze Tool and Slide Shape by QuicKutz; Scissors; Paper Cutter

INSTRUCTIONS

1. Stamp Photographs Phrase in Onyx Black and Cloud White over red cardstock and set ink with heat tool.
2. Cut and mat stamped cardstock onto folded black card.
3. Distress old dictionary text with Coffee ink; cut and mat along left side of card as shown.
4. Stamp Photographs Phrase in Onyx Black, overlapping image onto both papers.
5. Adhere black inspiration tape along center of card.
6. Create three black slide die cuts using Squeeze Tool by QuicKutz.
7. Stamp Boys in Onyx Black onto cream cardstock and trim images to fit behind slide die cuts.
8. Adhere slides to card as shown.
9. Stamp Camera in black ink onto cream cardstock.
10. Trim image and distress edges with Coffee ink; mat onto black cardstock.
11. Attach clip along top and adhere panel to card with Glue Dots.

TIPS
- Try moving around images and papers until satisfied with card appearance before adhering in place.
- Paint chips can be found at hardware and home improvement stores. There are countless shade options within each color family.

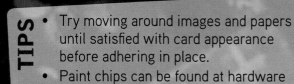

Two for Five Cents

ROBEN-MARIE SMITH

MATERIALS

Rubber Stamps: Numbers and Post Mark by Limited Edition

Dye Inkpads: StâzOn (Jet Black) by Tsukineko

Papers: Old Containers Paper by K&Company; Dictionary Thoughts Paper and Brown Distressed Cardstock by Pebbles, Inc.; Meaning Paper by Rusty Pickle; Ivory Crackle Paper (unkown); Tan Cardstock

Embellishments: Label Sticker by K&Company; Crow Clip Art; Vintage Image from Collage Sheet by Paperbag Studios; Black Button; Postage Stamp

Adhesives: Glue Stick; Glue Dots by Glue Dots International

Tools: Scissors; Paper Cutter

TECHNIQUE

- *Collage with Ephemera*

INSTRUCTIONS

1. Create card from Brown Distressed cardstock; cut and mat Ivory Crackle paper and tan cardstock onto card.
2. Stamp Numbers and Post Mark in Jet Black as shown.
3. Tear pieces from Dictionary Thoughts and Meaning papers.
4. Layer crow clip art under torn papers and adhere.
5. Cut images from Collage Sheet and Old Containers papers; layer images and adhere.
6. Add label sticker, postage stamp and button for embellishment.

Live Life Girl

LOUISE KOLKER

MATERIALS

Rubber Stamps: Live Life by Paperbag Studios; Ornament Background by Magenta; Phrases from No. 7 Sheet by Paperbag Studios

Pigment Inkpads: VersaMark Watermark (Clear) by Tsukineko

Dye Inkpads: StâzOn (Jet Black) by Tsukineko; Adirondack (Ginger) by Ranger

Papers: Terra Cotta; Cream and Black Cardstock; Old Dictionary Text; Old Bible Text

Embellishments: Orange Ribbon; Mini Black Frame Die Cuts; Plastic Slides

Adhesives: Glue Stick; Mod Podge Decoupage by Plaid; Glue Dots by Glue Dots International

Other: Paint Chips

Tools: Embossing Heat Tool; Die Cut Squeeze Tool and Mini Frame Shape by QuicKutz; Scissors; Paper Cutter

TECHNIQUES

- *Invisible Stamping* • *Collage with Ephemera*

INSTRUCTIONS

1. Stamp Ornament Background in Clear Versamark over terra cotta cardstock and set ink with heat tool.
2. Cut and mat onto black and cream cardstock; adhere to folded black card.
3. Cover three plastic slides with old dictionary text using Mod Podge and allow drying time.
4. Distress slides using Ginger ink.
5. Color plain cream cardstock with Ginger ink and over stamp Phrases in Jet Black.
6. Cut out individual images and adhere along bottom of slides.
7. Stamp Live Life in Jet Black onto various paint chips and set ink with heat tool.
8. Trim images to fit behind slides and adhere in place.
9. Cut strip from old Bible text and distress using Ginger ink.
10. Cut strip of black cardstock and glue orange ribbon and old Bible text in center.
11. Adhere strip panel in center of card and attach slides in place with Glue Dots.
12. Create mini black frame die cuts using Squeeze Tool by QuicKutz.
13. Add frames in between slides for embellishment.

Note: Journey card by Louise Kolker is made using the Collage with Ephemera technique. All rubber stamps are by Magenta.

TIPS

- Transparencies are best attached to cards with brads, snaps or clear-drying adhesives.
- Sobo Fabric glue is an effective adhesive to use on ribbons and fabrics because it dries clear and does not saturate fabric.

Every Life Has a Story

ROBEN-MARIE SMITH

TECHNIQUES
- *Transparancies on Top*
- *Collage with Ephemera*

MATERIALS

Rubber Stamps: The Story and No. 451921 by Paperbag Studios

Dye Inkpads: StâzOn (Jet Black) by Tsukineko

Papers: Brianna Red Damask and Green Gingham Papers by K&Company; Alpha Pistachio Paper by BasicGrey; Black Cardstock

Embellishments: Transparency by K&Company; Black Snaps

Adhesives: Glue Stick

Tools: 1/8" Hole Punch; Deckle Scissors by Fiskars; Scissors; Paper Cutter

INSTRUCTIONS

1. Stamp The Story in Jet Black onto Alpha Pistachio paper.
2. Cut around image with deckle scissors and mat onto black cardstock.
3. Cut and mat plain Alpha Pistachio paper onto black cardstock.
4. Adhere stamped panel as shown.
5. Stamp No. 451921 in Jet Black along side.
6. Trim transparency to size and layer over panel; punch holes in each corner for snap placement.
7. Insert snaps through holes, securing in back.
8. Mat onto Green Gingham and Brianna Red Damask papers; adhere to folded black card.

Children Believe

JILL HAGLUND

TECHNIQUE
- *Collage with Ephemera*

MATERIALS

Rubber Stamps: First Grade by Paperbag Studios

Pigment Inkpads: ColorBox Pigment (Cranberry and Lilac) by Clearsnap

Dye Inkpads: StâzOn (Jet Black) by Tsukineko

Papers: Textured Pink, Lavender, Purple and Green Cardstock; Cream Cardstock; Love Paper by 7gypsies

Colored Pencils: Red, Purple and Pink

Embellishments: Pewter Label Holder; Pewter Corners by Making Memories; Believe Button; Hand-Dyed Silk Ribbon

Adhesives: Glue Stick; Sobo Fabric Glue by Delta; Glue Dots by Glue Dots International

Tools: 1/8" Hole Punch; Scissors; Paper Cutter

INSTRUCTIONS

1. Stamp First Grade in Jet Black onto cream cardstock.
2. Highlight flower with colored pencils and cut out image.
3. Color edges of panel using Lilac pigment ink.
4. Mat onto textured pink, lavender, purple and green cardstock as shown.
5. Attach pewter corners with glue dots and adhere to folded green card.
6. Distress edges of card using Cranberry pigment ink.
7. Punch holes for brad placement.
8. Trim Love paper to fit behind label holder and adhere in place.
9. Thread ribbon through label holder, insert brads and attach to card.
10. Wrap ribbon around back and inside of card and adhere with fabric glue.

Note: Instructions for Vintage Girl card are on page 65.

What is now proved was once imagined.

looking back

TIPS

- Stamp a desired image twice; cut out parts of second image and adhere them over the first to create a three-dimensional look.

Looking Back
LOUISE KOLKER

MATERIALS

Rubber Stamps: Girl from Dream Notions Sheet by Paperbag Studios; Post Mark (unknown); Script (unknown)

Dye Inkpads: Tim Holtz Distress Ink (Tea Dye) and Adirondack (Rust and Espresso) by Ranger

Papers: Orange, Beige, Textured Brown and Glossy White Cardstock; Patterned Paper by Penny Black; Specialty Paper; Distressed Paper (unknown)

Embellishments: Brown Lace; Tan Photo Corners; Vintage Buttons; Pewter Phrase by Making Memories; Chip Board

Adhesives: Glue Stick; Tacky Glue; Mod Podge Decoupage by Plaid

Tools: Embossing Heat Tool; X-ACTO™ Knife; Cutting Mat; Ruler; Foam Brush; Scissors; Paper Cutter

TECHNIQUE
- *Collage with Ephemera*

INSTRUCTIONS

1. Stamp Girl in Rust onto glossy white cardstock; set ink with heat tool and set aside.
2. Tear piece of distressed paper and stamp Post Mark and Script in Espresso over paper.
3. Rub Tea Dye ink over images and adhere torn paper over beige cardstock panel.
4. Cut a rectangle of chipboard using X-ACTO™ knife and ruler over cutting mat.
5. Cover chipboard with orange specialty paper using Mod Podge and allow drying time.
6. Adhere beige cardstock panel in center of chipboard.
7. Attach tan photo corners to Girl image and adhere in place.
8. Add lace, buttons and pewter phrase for embellishment.
9. Mat chipboard piece onto textured brown cardstock.
10. Cut and mat Patterned paper and textured brown cardstock to folded orange card; adhere panel in center of card.

Emos and Everett
LOUISE KOLKER

MATERIALS

Rubber Stamps: Emos and Everett by River City Rubber Works; Artful Mosaic by Stampers Anonymous

Pigment Inkpads: ColorBox PetalPoint (Alchemy) by Clearsnap

Dye Inkpads: VersaFine (Onyx Black and Vintage Sepia) by Tsukineko

Papers: Orange, Green and Brown Cardstock; Specialty Paper

Embellishments: Ribbon with Snaps

Adhesives: Glue Stick; Diamond Glaze by JudiKins

Tools: Scissors; Paper Cutter

TECHNIQUES
- *Collage with Stamps*
- *Partial Image Design*

INSTRUCTIONS

1. Stamp Emos and Everett in Onyx Black onto orange cardstock.
2. Cut out individual images and mat onto green cardstock.
3. Repeat step one and cut out individual buttons from images; adhere to panels with adhesive foam tape.
4. Stamp Artful Mosaic in Vintage Sepia onto plain orange cardstock; cut and mat onto folded green card.
5. Ink Artful Mosaic in a copper shade from the PetalPoint and stamp onto brown cardstock.
6. Cut into strip and mat onto specialty paper and green cardstock; adhere in center of card.
7. Trim strip of ribbon and adhere onto orange cardstock; mat in center of panel.
8. Attach Emos and Everett panels as shown with adhesive foam tape.

MATERIALS

Rubber Stamps: Children's Feet from Imagined Sheet by Paperbag Studios; French Writing by Hero Arts

Dye Inkpads: StâzOn (Jet Black) by Tsukineko; Archival Ink (Maroon) by Ranger

Papers: Green, Black and White Cardstock; Pink Floral Paper (unknown); Polka Dot and Pistachio Paper by BasicGrey

Pastels/Chalks: Red, Yellow, Blue, Brown and Flesh Toned Chalks

Embellishments: Black Mini Brads by Making Memories; Pewter Flower

Adhesives: Glue Stick; Tacky Glue

Other: Post-It® Notes or Removable Tape; Spray Fixative

Tools: 1/8" Hole Punch; Cotton Swabs; Scissors; Paper Cutter

Children's feet
ROBEN-MARIE SMITH

INSTRUCTIONS

1. Stamp Children's Feet in Jet Black onto white cardstock.
2. Use the Paper Masking technique (pg 8) to hide image with Post-It® Notes.
3. Over stamp French Writing in Maroon around masked image.
4. Remove mask and color image with chalks using cotton swabs.
5. Spray chalked artwork with fixative and allow drying time.
6. Cut out artwork and adhere to panel of pink floral paper; mat onto black cardstock as shown.
7. Tear strip from Pistachio paper and adhere in place.
8. Punch holes for brad placement and attach black mini brads and pewter flower.
9. Cut and mat Polka Dot paper onto folded green card; adhere panel to card.

Vintage Girl

JILL HAGLUND

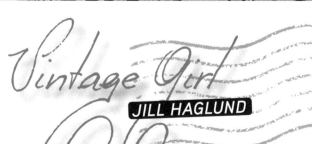

TECHNIQUE
• Collage with Ephemera

MATERIALS

Rubber Stamps: Large Cancellation by Stampington & Co.

Papers: Red, Green, Brown, Black and Cream Cardstock; Script Paper

Markers/Pens: Red, Green and Brown Brush Markers

Embellishments: Vintage Girl Image; Pewter Frame by Making Memories

Adhesives: Glue Stick; Tacky Glue

Tools: Scissors; Paper Cutter

INSTRUCTIONS

1. Color Large Cancellation stamp using brush markers, blending colors together.
2. Stamp onto cream cardstock.
3. Cut and mat image onto red and black cardstock.
4. Trim vintage girl image to fit behind pewter frame and adhere in place.
5. Mat panel onto script paper and brown cardstock; adhere to folded green card.

65

Grace
LINDA BROWN

MATERIALS

Rubber Stamps: Martha, French Correspondence, Diamond Avenue, Trois Femmes and Corner Décor by B Line Designs; Words in Diamonds by Postmodern Design; Alphabet by Hero Arts

Pigment Inkpads: VersaMagic (Cornucopia, Spanish Olive and Jumbo Java) and Encore! Ultimate Metallic (Gold) by Tsukineko

Dye Inkpads: Tim Holtz Distress Ink (Tea Dye) by Ranger

Papers: Cream Cardstock; Vintage Collage Paper by K&Company

Pastels/Chalks: Orange, Yellow, Green, Pink and Flesh Toned Chalks

Markers/Pens: Gold Leafing Pen by Krylon

Embellishments: Transparencies by Design Originals; Alphabet Tiles and Square Brads by All My Memories; Gold Key, Lock Charm and Corners by Fancifuls; Ornate Plaques by Collage Keepsakes; Gold Fibers; Beads; Gold and White Sheer Ribbon; Green Glitter Rickrack; String Pearls; White Buttons; Crystal Rhinestones; Paper Doilies

Adhesives: Glossy Accents by Ranger; Mod Podge Decoupage by Plaid; Glue Stick; Tacky Glue

Other: Quad Slide Mailer and Microscope Slides by Anima Designs

Tools: Embossing Heat Tool; Makeup Sponges; Small Stipple Brush; Cotton Swabs; Scissors; Paper Cutter

INSTRUCTIONS

Front Cover:

1. Cover the slide mailer in Cornucopia ink using makeup sponge and stipple brush; set ink with heat tool.
2. Repeat step one for thorough coverage.
3. Apply Spanish Olive and Jumbo Java inks over Cornucopia using sponge, blending colors together. Set ink with heat tool.
4. Stamp French Correspondence in Jumbo Java onto front cover.
5. Tear Vintage Collage paper and adhere along left side.
6. Over stamp Corner Décor in Gold covering script and paper.
7. Stamp Diamond Avenue three times in Jumbo Java onto cream cardstock; cut out images and adhere.
8. Adhere strip of gold sheer ribbon along bottom.
9. Stamp Martha in Jumbo Java onto cream cardstock.
10. Color with chalks using cotton swabs and tear around image.
11. Rub Gold pigment ink along edge and adhere in place.
12. Attach alphabet tiles, ornate plaques, string pearls, rickrack, gold key and buttons for embellishment.

Inside Card:

1. Stamp French Correspondence in Jumbo Java over inside cover.
2. Tear Vintage Collage paper and distress edges with dye ink; adhere in place.
3. Stamp Words in Diamonds over inside cover in Gold pigment ink and set with heat tool.
4. Distress doilies with dye ink, trim and adhere along top.
5. Stamp Diamond Avenue in Jumbo Java onto cream cardstock.
6. Cut out image and adhere in center.
7. Adhere corners along top and bottom of diamond image.
8. Stamp Trois Femmes in Jumbo Java onto cream cardstock; cut out image and highlight with chalks.
9. Apply Gold pigment ink around edge and adhere in center of diamond.
10. String beads onto gold fibers and wrap around fold of card, securing at the bottom. Attach sheer white ribbon in similar fashion.
11. Adhere individual collages to cream cardstock and layer under microscope slides.
12. Cut off excess paper and adhere collage to slide with Glossy Accents.
13. Edge slides in gold leafing pen and adhere.

Napoleon

LOUISE KOLKER

MATERIALS

Rubber Stamps: Napoleon and Missive Clock by Lynne Perrella for Acey Deucy; Binding Edge by Stampers Anonymous; Small Butterflies, Paris Eyes and Hand (unknown)

Dye Inkpads: StâzOn (Jet Black and Timber Brown) by Tsukineko; Adirondack (Butterscotch, Terra Cotta and Ginger) and Archival Ink (Mustard) by Ranger

Papers: Orange, Dark Orange, Black and Glossy White Cardstock

Markers/Pens: Light Blue, Dark Blue, Brown and Tan Brush Markers; Dotta-Riffic Marker (Black) by Zig

Embellishments: Black Inspiration Tape by Club Scrap

Adhesives: Glue Stick; Adhesive Foam Tape

Other: Post-It® Notes or Removable Tape

Tools: Makeup Sponge; Embossing Heat Tool; Scissors; Paper Cutter

TECHNIQUES

- Paper Masking
- Direct-to-Glossy Paper with Dye Ink
- Collage with Stamps

INSTRUCTIONS

1. Stamp Napoleon in Jet Black onto glossy white cardstock.
2. Use the Paper Masking technique (pg 8) to hide image with Post-It® Notes.
3. Over stamp collage of images in black ink as shown and set with heat tool.
4. Sponge over mask with dye inks starting with Mustard in the center and moving outwards with darker colors.
5. Remove mask and color Napoleon image with markers as shown.
6. Stamp Small Butterflies on plain sheet of glossy white cardstock.
7. Set ink with heat tool and color with markers.
8. Cut out individual images and adhere center of butterflies with adhesive foam tape, folding wings up for dimension.
9. Create splatter dots with Dotta-Riffic marker.
10. Cut and mat artwork onto black, dark orange, and black cardstock as shown. Adhere panels to folded orange card.
11. Attach inspiration tape along edge of card.

TIPS
- When using the Dotta-Riffic marker, press harder for large splatter and softly for small spots.

Time

JILL HAGLUND

MATERIALS

Rubber Stamps: Autumn by Lynne Perrella for Acey Deucy; Alphabet by Hero Arts; Clock (unknown)

Dye Inkpads: StâzOn (Jet Black and Timber Brown) by Tsukineko

Papers: Blue, Gold and Black Cardstock

Colored Pencils: Blue, Green, Orange and White

Adhesives: Glue Stick

Tools: Paper Cutter

TECHNIQUE

- Collage with Stamps

INSTRUCTIONS

1. Stamp Autumn and Clock in Timber Brown onto gold cardstock as shown.
2. Color around images with various colored pencils; highlight clocks with white.
3. Stamp phrase in Jet Black using alphabet stamps.
4. Cut and mat artwork onto blue cardstock; adhere to folded black card.

*A*vant-garde (uh-vahnt-gahrd) –noun, adj.: French origin; pertaining to the experimental treatment of literary, musical or artistic works. Describing something as unorthodox, daring or radical.

Avant-garde represents a pushing of boundaries that are accepted as the norm or status quo. Used here, it refers to works that are experimental or novel in form. This chapter features eccentric designs with artistic flair—avant-garde in appearance and technique. Go ahead... take a walk on the wild side. You may be surprised where it will lead!

"*'I think I could, if I only knew how to begin.' For, you see, so many out-of-the-way things had happened lately that Alice had begun to think that very few things indeed were really impossible.*"

~ *Alice in Wonderland by Lewis Carroll*

Frida Kahlo
JILL HAGLUND

MATERIALS

Rubber Stamps: Frida by Stampotique Originals; Flower Border by Christine Adolph for Stampington & Co.

Dye Inkpads: StâzOn (Jet Black) by Tsukineko

Papers: White Cardstock; Striped Patterned Paper

Pastels/Chalks: Flesh Toned Chalk

Colored Pencils: Red, Yellow and Green

Embellishments: Silk Flower; Metal Frame; Green Mini Brads

Adhesives: Glue Stick

Other: Computer

Tools: 1/8" Hole Punch; Cotton Swabs; Scissors; Paper Cutter

TECHNIQUE
- *Collage with Stamps*

INSTRUCTIONS

1. Stamp Frida in Jet Black onto white cardstock.
2. Color face with flesh toned chalk using cotton swabs.
3. Highlight with colored pencils and cut out image.
4. Stamp edges of folded white card with Flower Border in black ink.
5. Cut and mat striped paper in center of card.
6. Adhere stamped image to card and attach silk flower for embellishment.
7. Computer-generate "Frida", print onto white paper and cut to fit behind metal frame.
8. Punch holes for brad placement; adhere "Frida" behind frame and attach to card with brads as shown.

Photos
JILL HAGLUND

MATERIALS

Rubber Stamps: Modern Woman, Photos and Antique Border by Stampotique Originals; Dots by Hot Potatoes

Pigment Inkpads: ColorBox PetalPoint (Primary and Aurora) by Clearsnap

Dye Inkpads: StâzOn (Jet Black) by Tsukineko

Papers: White Cardstock

Tools: Paper Cutter

TECHNIQUE
- *Collage with Stamps*

INSTRUCTIONS

1. Stamp Dots over folded white card in variety of shades from the PetalPoints.
2. Over stamp Modern Woman and Photos in Jet Black as shown.
3. Stamp Antique Border along edge of card.

Note: Thank You card by Jill Haglund is made using the Collage with Stamps technique. All rubber stamps by Stampotique Originals.

Yellow Pears
JILL HAGLUND

MATERIALS

Rubber Stamps: Pears (Image), Pears (Word) and Script by A Stamp In The Hand

Pigment Inkpads: ColorBox Pigment (Orange) by Clearsnap

Dye Inkpads: Adirondack (Sepia) by Ranger

Papers: Green Striped Paper; Green, Ivory and Glossy White Cardstock

Markers/Pens: Orange, Yellow, Green and Brown Water-Based Markers; Gold Leafing Pen by Krylon; Glitter Pen

Adhesives: Glue Stick

Tools: Stipple Brush; Paper Cutter

TECHNIQUES
- *Stipple Art*
- *Stamping in Marker onto Glossy Paper*

INSTRUCTIONS

1. Stamp Pears (word) and Script in Sepia ink onto folded ivory card.
2. Cut and tear green striped paper and adhere to card.
3. Trim green cardstock into thin strip and adhere over green striped paper.
4. Color Pears (image) with markers, blending inks, and stamp onto glossy white cardstock. Color and stamp again.
5. Stipple over pears in orange pigment ink.
6. Cut and mat image onto card as shown.
7. Edge right side of card with gold leafing pen.
8. Use glitter pen along bottom of pear panel and allow drying time.

TIPS
- Marvy water-based markers are well known for coloring stamps because of rich colors and generous ink supply, which add brilliance to stamped images.

Art Friends
ROBEN-MARIE SMITH

MATERIALS

Rubber Stamps: Flower and Girl by Paperbag Studios; 282 Dial by Treasure Cay

Dye Inkpads: StâzOn (Jet Black) by Tsukineko

Papers: Light Green, Dark Green and White Cardstock; Fleur Rouge Paper by 7gypsies; Art Paper by Rusty Pickle

Colored Pencils: Red, Yellow and Flesh Toned

Embellishments: Black Mini Brads by Making Memories; Alphabet Tile

Adhesives: Glue Stick; Tacky Glue

Tools: 1/8" Hole Punch; Label Maker; Scissors; Paper Cutter

TECHNIQUE
- *Collage with Ephemera*

INSTRUCTIONS

1. Cut, tear and adhere light green cardstock, Fleur Rouge and Art paper onto folded dark green card.
2. Stamp 282 Dial in Jet Black over art paper as shown.
3. Create "Friends" label from label maker and adhere to card.
4. Stamp Flower and Girl in black ink onto white cardstock.
5. Color image with colored pencils, cut out and adhere to card.
6. Punch holes for brad placement and attach black mini brads.

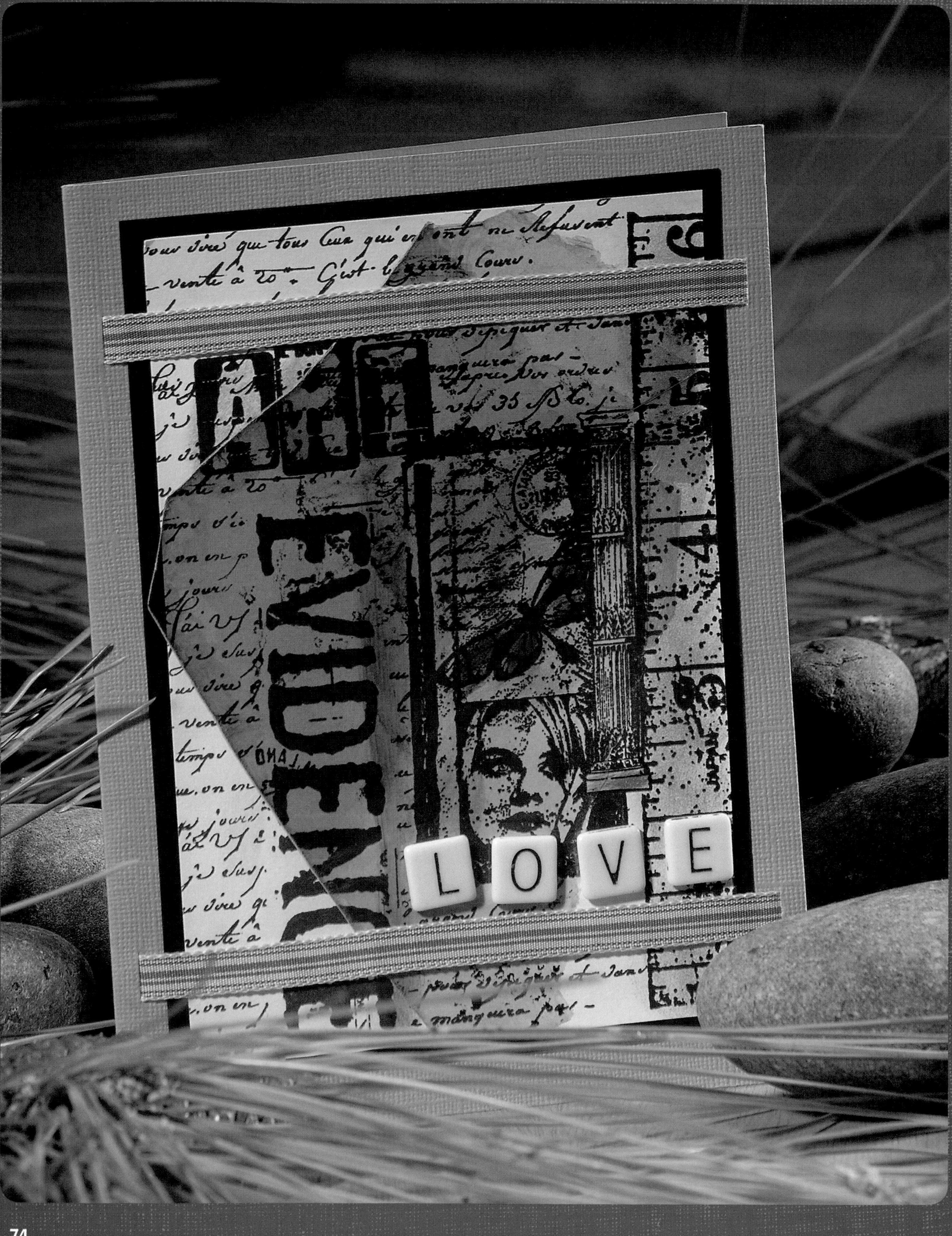
LOVE

Aspire to Be
JILL HAGLUND

MATERIALS

Rubber Stamps: Leaf by Personal Stamp Exchange; Aspire to Be by Dawn Houser for Inkadinkado; Moon by Magenta

Pigment Inkpads: ColorBox PetalPoint (Arboretum) by Clearsnap

Dye Inkpads: StâzOn (Jet Black) by Tsukineko; Adirondack (Meadow and Cranberry) by Ranger

Papers: Red, Green and Cream Cardstock; Green Patterned Paper; Sheet Music

Embellishments: Green Ribbon; Gold Heart Charm; Butterfly Image

Adhesives: Glue Stick; Double-Sided Tape

Other: Gold Wire

TECHNIQUE
• *Collage with Ephemera*

INSTRUCTIONS

1. Tear around butterfly image; mat onto red and green cardstock and green patterned paper as shown. Tear patterned paper along edge for textured look.
2. Tear sheet music and mat onto folded cream card.
3. Adhere butterfly panel to card.
4. Over stamp Leaf in Meadow, Moon in Cranberry and Aspire to Be in Jet Black.
5. Ink edge of card in purple and green shades from the PetalPoint.
6. Tie ribbon around fold of card creating bow in front.
7. String charm onto gold wire and attach to bow.

Note: Aspire to Be card is pictured on page 72.

TIPS
• Old encyclopedias are a creative resource for ephemera.

Evidence of Love
WAYNE DIELEMAN

MATERIALS

Rubber Stamps: Ruler, Art, Evidence, Column Collage and Dutch Script by Stampers Anonymous

Pigment Inkpads: ColorBox PetalPoint (Provence) by Clearsnap

Dye Inkpads: StâzOn (Jet Black) by Tsukineko

Papers: , Black, White and Textured Orange Cardstock

Embellishments: Alphabet Tiles; Orange Ribbon; Mica

Adhesives: Glue Stick; Tacky Glue; Diamond Glaze by JudiKins

Tools: Embossing Heat Tool; Scissors; Paper Cutter

TECHNIQUES
• *Direct-to-Paper with Ink*
• *Collage with Stamps*

INSTRUCTIONS

1. Stamp collage of images in Jet Black ink onto white cardstock.
2. Color images with the Direct-to-Paper technique (pg 13) using variety of shades from the PetalPoint; set ink with heat tool.
3. Cut and mat artwork onto black cardstock; adhere to folded orange card.
4. Cut and adhere mica to card with Diamond Glaze.
5. Attach ribbon and alphabet tiles as shown using tacky glue.

TIPS
• Be sure to use clear-drying adhesive when attaching mica to cards.

Butterfly Kisses
SANDY HUBER

MATERIALS

Rubber Stamps: Butterfly (unknown); Butterfly Kisses by Rubbermoon Stamp Company

Pigment Inkpads: ColorBox Pigment (Brown) by Clearsnap

Dye Inkpads: StâzOn (Jet Black) by Tsukineko

Embossing Powders: Clear

Papers: Brown and Tan Cardstock; Flower Paper by BasicGrey

Markers/Pens: Glitter Pen

Adhesives: Glue Stick; Adhesive Foam Tape

Tools: Embossing Heat Tool; Scissors; Paper Cutter

TECHNIQUE
• Layering Stamped Images

INSTRUCTIONS

1. Stamp Butterfly in Brown onto brown cardstock; apply embossing powder and emboss with heat tool.
2. Cut out complete image from brown cardstock.
3. Stamp Butterfly three times in Brown onto tan cardstock.
4. Apply embossing powder and emboss images with heat tool.
5. Cut out partial images from each Butterfly on tan cardstock, graduating from smaller to larger pieces.
6. Outline wings using glitter pen and allow glitter to dry thoroughly.
7. Layer each image and adhere with adhesive foam tape in center, folding up wings for dimension.
8. Create card from Flower paper, cutting around flower picture in front.
9. Outline flower picture using glitter pen and allow drying time; adhere Butterfly to card.
10. Stamp Butterfly Kisses in Jet Black along bottom of card.

Fuji Goddess
SANDY HUBER

MATERIALS

Rubber Stamps: Fuji Goddess by Lynne Perrella for Acey Deucy; Japanese Letters (unknown)

Pigment Inkpads: ColorBox Pigment (Red and Black) by Clearsnap

Embossing Powders: Clear

Dye Inkpads: StâzOn (Jet Black) by Tsukineko

Papers: Red Patterned Paper by BasicGrey; Japanese Text Paper

Embellishments: Gold Coins

Adhesives: Glue Stick; Tacky Glue

Other: Microscope Slides; Silver Foil Tape

Tools: Embossing Heat Tool; Decorative Corner Punch; Scissors; Paper Cutter

TECHNIQUE
• Microscope Slide Art

INSTRUCTIONS

1. Stamp Fuji Goddess in Jet Black onto Red Patterned paper and trim to fit behind slide.
2. Layer image between two microscope slides; use silver foil tape to seal around edges.
3. Adhere to panel of Red Patterned paper with tacky glue.
4. Use decorative corner punch on four corners of panel.
5. Create card using Red Patterned paper and adhere panel to top of card.
6. Stamp Japanese Letters in Black pigment ink onto Red Patterned paper; apply embossing powder and emboss with heat tool.
7. Trim around image and punch corners with decorative punch.
8. Tear Japanese text and color with red pigment ink.
9. Adhere Japanese Letters panel to inked text and attach to card as shown.
10. Glue coins in place for embellishment.
11. Punch four corners of card with decorative punch.

TIPS
• Microscope slides make beautiful embellishments for cards when layered over stamped images.

Butterfly Kisses...

All Night Long Look
JILL HAGLUND

MATERIALS

Rubber Stamps: Asian Woman by A Stamp In The Hand; Seals and Kanji Poem by Hero Arts; Calligraphy by Posh Impressions

Pigment Inkpads: ColorBox MetalExtra (Goldrush) and ColorBox PetalPoint (Arboretum and Mosaic) by Clearsnap

Dye Inkpads: StâzOn (Jet Black) by Tsukineko

Embossing Powders: Gold

Papers: Black Cardstock; Gold Corrugated Paper; Chinese/English Bible Text

Embellishments: Gold Coins; Fibers; Large Tag

Adhesives: Glue Stick; Tacky Glue

Tools: Embossing Heat Tool; Scissors; Paper Cutter

TECHNIQUES
- *Direct-to-Paper with Ink*
- *Collage with Ephemera*

INSTRUCTIONS

1. Stamp Calligraphy in Goldrush onto folded black card; apply embossing powder and emboss with heat tool.
2. Use Direct-to-Paper technique (pg 13) and variety of shades from PetalPoints to color tag.
3. Stamp collage of images in Jet Black onto tag as shown.
4. Tear piece of Chinese/English Bible text and layer between gold corrugated paper and inked tag; adhere papers to card.
5. Thread fibers through large gold coin and adhere coins to card with tacky glue.

TIPS
- Try layering Chinese/English Bible text to an Asian-themed card for a creative ephemera embellishment.

Standing Woman
JILL HAGLUND

MATERIALS

Rubber Stamps: Asian Woman by Lynne Perrella for Stampington & Co.; Trim by Christine Adolph for Stampington & Co.; Seals by Hero Arts

Pigment Inkpads: ColorBox PetalPoint (Arboretum and Mosaic) and Top Boss Embossing (Clear) by Clearsnap

Dye Inkpads: StâzOn (Jet Black) by Tsukineko

Embossing Powders: Ultra Thick (Clear)

Papers: Black and White Cardstock; Purple and Gold Corrugated Paper; Chinese/English Bible Text; Lace Specialty Paper

Embellishments: Gold Coin; Asian Postage Stamp

Adhesives: Glue Stick; Tacky Glue

Other: Shoebox

Tools: Embossing Heat Tool; Scissors; Paper Cutter

TECHNIQUES
- *Direct-to-Paper with Ink*
- *Ultra Thick Embossing*
- *Collage with Ephemera*

INSTRUCTIONS

1. Use Direct-to-Paper technique (pg 13) and variety of shades from PetalPoints to color panel of white cardstock.
2. Stamp Asian Woman and Seals in Jet Black over inked cardstock.
3. Tear piece of Chinese/English Bible text and adhere to folded black card; cut and layer gold and purple corrugated papers and lace specialty paper as shown.
4. Stamp Trim in Jet Black onto white cardstock and cut to desired size.
5. Adhere stamped panels on top of papers.
6. Cover postage stamp in Clear pigment ink and apply ultra thick embossing powder.
7. Place postage stamp in shoebox and emboss with heat tool.
7. Adhere postage stamp and gold coin to card as shown.

TIPS
- Add style to your cards with authentic postage stamps.

Asian Icon

JILL HAGLUND

MATERIALS

Rubber Stamps: Asian Woman and Background Panel by A Stamp In The Hand; Seals by Hero Arts; Flower Icon by CC Rubber Stamps

Pigment Inkpads: ColorBox PetalPoint (Arboretum and Mosaic) by Clearsnap

Dye Inkpads: StâzOn (Jet Black) by Tsukineko

Papers: White Cardstock; Specialty Paper

Embellishments: Gold Coin; Fibers; Bamboo Sticks

Adhesives: Glue Stick; Tacky Glue

Other: Post-It® Notes or Removable Tape; Thin Gold Wire

Tools: Scissors; Wire Cutter; Paper Cutter

TECHNIQUES

- *Direct-to-Paper with Ink*
- *Collage with Ephemera*
- *Paper Masking*

INSTRUCTIONS

1. Stamp Background Panel in purple shade from the PetalPoint onto folded white card and distress edges of card.
2. Stamp Seals in Jet Black over card.
3. Cut and adhere specialty paper to card as shown.
4. Use Direct-to-Paper technique (pg 13) and variety of shades from PetalPoints to color panel of white cardstock.
5. Stamp Asian Woman in Jet Black over inked cardstock.
6. Use the Paper Masking technique (pg 8) to hide image with Post-It® Notes.
7. Over stamp Background Panel in black ink and remove mask.
8. Stamp Flower Icon in black ink over stamped cardstock; adhere panel to card.
9. Wrap bamboo sticks in thin gold wire and attach to card with tacky glue.
10. Thread fibers through gold coin and add for embellishment.

Dragonfly Art Print

JILL HAGLUND

MATERIALS

Rubber Stamps: Flower Background by SonLight Impressions; Dragonfly Art Print by Hero Arts

Pigment Inkpads: ColorBox MetalExtra (Goldrush) by Clearsnap

Dye Inkpads: StâzOn (Jet Black) by Tsukineko

Embossing Powders: Gold

Papers: Red, Black, White and Metallic Gold Cardstock; Gold Corrugated Paper; Specialty Paper

Colored Pencils: Red, Green, Blue and Purple

Markers/Pens: Gold Leafing Pen by Krylon

Embellishments: Gold Coin; Fibers

Adhesives: Glue Stick; Tacky Glue

Tools: Decorative Corner Punch; Scissors; Paper Cutter

TECHNIQUE

- *Collage with Ephemera*

INSTRUCTIONS

1. Stamp Dragonfly Art Print in Jet Black onto white cardstock.
2. Highlight images with colored pencils and trim to size.
3. Punch four corners with decorative punch and edge panel with gold leafing pen.
4. Mat panel onto black, metallic gold and black cardstock as shown and set aside.
5. Stamp Flower Background in Goldrush onto folded red card; apply embossing powder and emboss with heat tool.
6. Cut and adhere specialty paper and gold corrugated paper to card.
7. Thread fibers through gold coin and add for embellishment.
8. Adhere dragonfly panel to card.

Note: Woman in Wind card by Jill Haglund is made using the Collage with Ephemera technique. Rubber Stamp by Hero Arts.

Blue Fish Legend

WAYNE DIELEMAN

MATERIALS

Rubber Stamps: Ruler and Fish Legend by Stampers Anonymous

Dye Inkpads: StâzOn (Jet Black) by Tsukineko

Papers: White and Textured Blue Cardstock; Cardigan Paper by Scrapbookpaper

Pastels/Chalks: Blue and Purple Chalks

Embellishments: Blue Mini Brads by Making Memories; Pewter Fish Charms

Adhesives: Glue Stick; Adhesive Foam Tape

Other: Spray Fixative

Tools: 1/8" Hole Punch; Cotton Swabs; Scissors; Paper Cutter

TECHNIQUES
- *Collage with Stamps*
- *Coloring with Chalks*

INSTRUCTIONS

1. Stamp Fish Legend in Jet Black onto white cardstock.
2. Color fish with chalks using cotton swabs and spray with fixative; cut around image and set aside.
3. Stamp Ruler in Jet Black onto textured blue cardstock twice and cut out images.
4. Cut and mat Blue Cardigan paper onto white cardstock; adhere to folded blue card.
5. Attach Ruler images along top and bottom of card using adhesive foam tape.
6. Mat fish panel to blue and white cardstock, tearing cardstock along bottom; adhere to center of card.
7. Punch holes for brad placement and attach pewter fish charms to card with blue mini brads as shown.

Green Skeletal Fish

WAYNE DIELEMAN

MATERIALS

Rubber Stamps: Skeletal Fish, Ruler and Binding Edge by Stampers Anonymous; Alphabet by Hero Arts; Small Fish by Magenta

Dye Inkpads: StâzOn (Jet Black) by Tsukineko

Papers: Dark Green and Ivory Cardstock; Script Paper

Pastels/Chalks: Orange Chalk

Markers/Pens: Yellow, Green and Blue Water-Based Markers

Embellishments: Ribbon and Fibers; Sticker Tags; Black Mini Brads by Making Memories; Green Fine Weave Magic Mesh by Magic Mesh

Adhesives: Glue Stick; Tacky Glue

Tools: 1/8" Hole Punch; Embossing Heat Tool; Water Bottle; Cotton Swabs; Scissors; Paper Cutter

TECHNIQUES
- *Faux Watercolor with Marker and Dye Ink*
- *Collage with Stamps*

INSTRUCTIONS

1. Color Skeletal Fish stamp with markers as shown and rub Jet Black ink along edge.
2. Lightly spritz inked stamp with water and press onto ivory cardstock. Use heat tool to dry image.
3. Stamp Binding Edge in black ink along top.
4. Tear around images and set artwork aside.
5. Stamp Ruler and Small Fish in Jet Black onto ivory cardstock and color Ruler with orange chalk using cotton swab. Cut out both images and set aside.
6. Stamp Ruler in Jet Black along top and bottom of folded dark green card.
7. Layer green Magic Mesh, torn script paper and fish panel onto card and adhere in place.
8. Attach colored Ruler and Small Fish images to card as shown.
9. Wrap ribbon and fibers around card and tie along fold.
10. Stamp tag stickers with Alphabet stamps in Jet Black and adhere onto fish panel.
11. Punch holes for brad placement and attach mini brads.

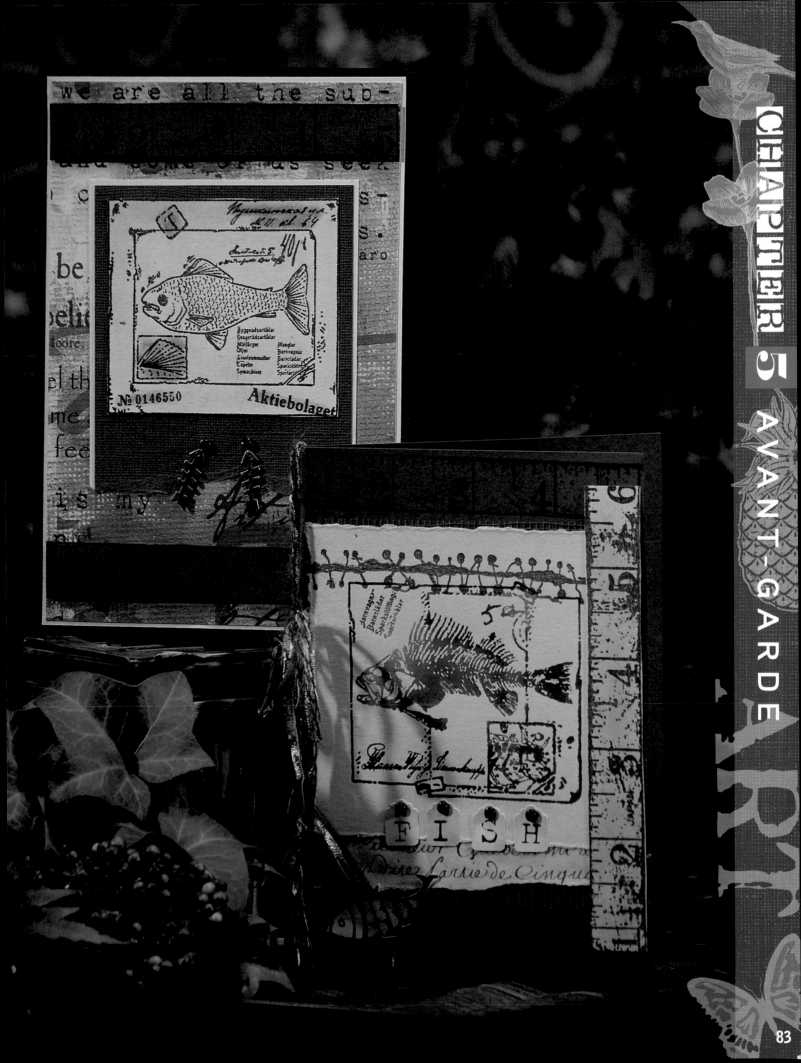

Gracious Lady
LOUISE KOLKER

MATERIALS

Rubber Stamps: Gracious Lady, Style is Eternal and Skyland Bookmark by Hero Arts

Dye Inkpads: StâzOn (Jet Black and Timber Brown) by Tsukineko; Adirondack (Butterscotch, Terra Cotta and Ginger) and Archival Ink (Mustard) by Ranger

Papers: Orange, Black, White and Glossy White Cardstock

Adhesives: Glue Stick; Tape

Other: Post-It® Notes or Removable Tape; Box Tile Template by Tamp-A-Stamp

Tools: Embossing Heat Tool; Makeup Sponge; Paper Cutter

TECHNIQUE
• *Direct-to-Glossy Paper with Dye Ink*

INSTRUCTIONS

1. Tape box tile template onto glossy cardstock.
2. Sponge over template with dye inks starting with Mustard in the center and moving outwards with darker colors.
3. Remove template and set ink with heat tool.
4. Use the Paper Masking technique (pg 8) to isolate upper left and lower right tiles using Post-It® Notes.
5. Stamp Style is Eternal in Jet Black over inked tiles.
6. Remove masks and isolate upper right and lower left tiles.
7. Stamp Skyland Bookmark in black ink over tiles and remove masks.
8. Isolate center tile with masks and stamp Gracious Lady in Jet Black.
9. Set ink with heat tool.
10. Cut and mat artwork onto black, orange and white cardstock; adhere to folded black card.

People See Only...
LOUISE KOLKER

MATERIALS

Rubber Stamps: Prepared to See (Man), Reward Phrase and Numbers by Paperbag Studios; Oval Frame (unknown)

Pigment Inkpads: Opalite Pigment (Winter Rust) by Tsukineko

Dye Inkpads: StâzOn (Jet Black) by Tsukineko

Papers: Brown, Black, Ivory and Shimmer Gold Cardstock; Dictionary Text

Markers/Pens: Gold Leafing Pen by Krylon; Brown and Tan Brush Markers

Embellishments: Gold Brads; Brown Lace; Gold Tape; Acrylic Oval

Adhesives: Tacky Glue; Double-Sided Tape

Other: Post-It® Notes or Removable Tape

Tools: Drill; Label Maker; Scissors; Paper Cutter

TECHNIQUES
• *Paper Masking*
• *Collage with Ephemera*

INSTRUCTIONS

1. Stamp Numbers in Winter Rust onto brown cardstock; cut and mat onto folded black card.
2. Attach brown lace to panel of gold shimmer cardstock; adhere on top of brown cardstock.
3. Stamp Reward Phrase in Jet Black onto gold tape and place in center of card between two cardstock panels.
4. Tear dictionary text and adhere in center of card.
5. Stamp Oval Frame in Jet Black onto ivory cardstock.
6. Use the Paper Masking technique (pg 8) to hide image with Post-It® Notes.
7. Stamp Prepared to See in black ink inside frame image.
8. Color images with brush markers as shown and cut around frame.
9. Drill small holes in acrylic oval and attach over stamped images with gold brads.
10. Create phrase with label maker and adhere to card.
11. Color edge of card and acrylic oval with gold leafing pen.

Art Hand in Heart
LOUISE KOLKER

MATERIALS

Rubber Stamps: Art Hand and Heart, Stone Spiral, Collage Cube, Swirls and Pear by Stampers Anonymous

Dye Inkpads: StâzOn (Jet Black and Royal Purple) by Tsukineko; Vivid! Dye Ink (Tea Rose and Lavender) by Clearsnap

Papers: Purple, Pink, Black, White and Glossy White Cardstock

Adhesives: Glue Stick; Adhesive Foam Tape

Tools: Embossing Heat Tool; Paper Cutter

TECHNIQUES
- *Collage with Stamps*
- *Direct-to-Glossy Paper with Dye Ink*

INSTRUCTIONS

1. Stamp collage of images in Jet Black onto purple cardstock.
2. Cut and mat onto pink cardstock; adhere to folded black card.
3. Stamp Collage Cube in Royal Purple onto glossy white cardstock; set ink with heat tool.
4. Rub Tea Rose and Lavender inks over image as shown.
5. Cut and mat onto white cardstock with adhesive foam tape.
6. Mat onto black and pink cardstock panel; adhere to center of card with adhesive foam tape.

Grow Child
AMY WELLENSTEIN

MATERIALS

Rubber Stamps: Child by Stampotique Originals

Dye Inkpads: StâzOn (Jet Black) by Tsukineko

Papers: Green, Purple, Black and White Cardstock; Green Patterned Paper

Pastels/Chalks: Yellow, Green, Pink and Flesh Toned Chalks

Embellishments: Grow Button by Li'l Davis Designs; Vintage Circle by K&Company

Adhesives: Glue Stick; Tacky Glue

Other: Spray Fixative

Tools: Cotton Balls; Cotton Swabs; Paper Cutter

TECHNIQUE
- *Collage with Ephemera*

INSTRUCTIONS

1. Stamp Child in Jet Black onto white cardstock.
2. Color over image with yellow chalk using cotton balls; shake off excess chalk.
3. Highlight child and flower with green, pink and flesh toned chalks using cotton swabs.
4. Spray with fixative and allow artwork to dry.
5. Cut and mat onto black and purple cardstock panels, layering as shown.
6. Cut and mat green patterned paper onto folded green card; adhere original artwork to card.
7. Finish card by adding embellishments.

Once Upon a Time in Paris

ROBEN-MARIE SMITH

MATERIALS

Rubber Stamps: Post Mark (unknown)

Dye Inkpads: StâzOn (Jet Black) by Tsukineko

Papers: Black Cardstock; Red Patterned Paper by 7gypsies

Embellishments: Transparency, Twill and Hardware by 7gypsies; Eiffel Tower Photo Print by ARTchix Studio; Letters by Li'l Davis Designs; White Ribbon; Black Brad

Adhesives: Glue Stick; Diamond Glaze by JudiKins

Tools: 1/8" Hole Punch; Label

TECHNIQUES

- *Collage with Ephemera*
- *Transparencies on Top*

INSTRUCTIONS

1. Cut Red Patterned paper to fit front of folded black card. Tear along edge and adhere.
2. Stamp Post Mark in Jet Black onto photo print and adhere to card.
3. Cut transparency and layer over Red Patterned paper and photo print; adhere with diamond glaze.
4. Attach hardware and black brad to twill.
5. Punch holes for hardware placement and attach as shown.
6. Create date using label maker and cut out individual numbers.
7. Adhere "Paris" and date over transparency.
8. Tie white ribbons around hardware and trim ends.

Note: Twill is fabric ribbon made by 7gypsies with printed phrases.

Eiffel Tower

PATTI MUMA

MATERIALS

Rubber Stamps: Eiffel Tower by Stampers Anonymous; Script (unknown); Paris (unknown)

Dye Inkpads: StâzOn (Jet Black and Timber Brown) by Tsukineko; Tim Holtz Distress Ink (Tea Dye) by Ranger

Papers: Ivory Cardstock; Coffee-Dyed Paper; White Paper; Brown Vellum

Embellishments: Copper Eyelets; Black Mini Brads by Making Memories

Adhesives: Glue Stick; Diamond Glaze by JudiKins

Other: Post-It® Notes or Removable Tape

Tools: Eyelet Setting Tool; 1/8" Hole Punch; Scissors; Paper Cutter

TECHNIQUES

- *Paper Masking*
- *Collage with Stamps*

INSTRUCTIONS

1. Stamp Eiffel Tower in Timber Brown onto ivory cardstock.
2. Use the Paper Masking technique (pg 8) to hide image with Post-It® Notes.
3. Over stamp Script in Timber Brown around masked image.
4. Remove mask; cut around image creating panel and distress edges with Tea Dye ink.
5. Cut and mat onto coffee-dyed paper.
6. Stamp Paris in Jet Black onto brown vellum.
7. Trim around image, layer over inked panel and punch holes for brad placement.
8. Attach black mini brads as shown.
9. Trim white paper creating strip and tear ends of strip.
10. Wrap paper strip around coffee-dyed panel and punch holes for eyelet placement.
11. Set copper eyelets as shown and adhere panel to folded ivory card.
12. Distress edges of card using Tea Dye ink.

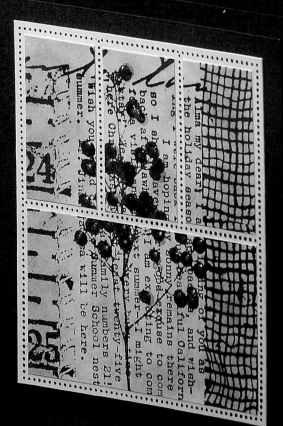

Every rubber stamper knows that holidays are perfect opportunities for inspiration in card making. This chapter focuses on two of our favorite holidays to celebrate with rubber stamped cards—Christmas and Valentine's Day. Friends and family will appreciate your homemade creations like no other, and inspire you to keep on stamping. Techniques featured include collage with ephemera, postage stamping, decoupage and much more.

Whether you are stamping secret Valentine messages or joyful Christmas expressions, pass them on to loved ones through your thoughtful designs.

One of the secrets of life is that all that is really worth doing is what we do for others.
~ Lewis Carroll

Christmas Angel

AMY WELLENSTEIN

MATERIALS

Rubber Stamps: Antique Music and Allegro Angel by Carin Andersson for Stampington & Co.; Italian Text by Rubber Baby Buggy Bumpers

Pigment Inkpads: VersaMark Watermark (Clear) and VersaFine (Onyx Black) by Tsukineko

Embossing Powders: Brass

Papers: Red, Green, Black, White and Ivory Cardstock

Pastels/Chalks: Red, Green, Blue and Flesh Toned Chalks

Colored Pencils: Red, Yellow and Blue

Adhesives: Glue Stick

Tools: Embossing Heat Tool; Cotton Swabs; Scissors; Paper Cutter

TECHNIQUES
- Coloring with Chalks
- Invisible Stamping

INSTRUCTIONS

1. Stamp Allegro Angel in Onyx Black onto white cardstock. Set ink with heat tool and cut out image.
2. Color image with chalks using cotton swabs. Highlight eyes, lips and headband with colored pencil.
3. Ink edge of image with Clear Watermark, apply embossing powder and emboss with heat tool.
4. Stamp Italian Text in black ink onto red cardstock. Tear around edges and adhere chalk artwork in center.
5. Stamp Antique Music in Clear Watermark onto green cardstock and set with heat tool.
6. Cut and mat onto black cardstock; adhere to folded ivory card.
7. Adhere stamped panel in center of card.

TECHNIQUES
- Coloring with Chalks
- Postage Stamping

Happy Holidays Post

AMY WELLENSTEIN

MATERIALS

Rubber Stamps: Happy and Holidays by Stampotique Originals; Berry Print by Christine Adolph for Stampington & Co.; Mesh Border by Stampington & Co.; Postage Blank by Just For Fun

Pigment Inkpads: VersaFine (Onyx Black) by Tsukineko

Papers: Red, Green and White Cardstock

Pastels/Chalks: Orange, Green and Pink Chalks

Colored Pencils: Red

Adhesives: Glue Stick

Other: Crystal Lacquer by Sakura Hobby Craft; Spray Fixative

Tools: Cotton Swabs; Scissors; Paper Cutter

INSTRUCTIONS

1. Stamp Berry Print and Mesh Border in Onyx Black onto white cardstock.
2. Color images with chalks using cotton swabs. Highlight berries with red colored pencil.
3. Spray artwork with fixative and allow drying time.
4. Use Postage Blank stamp and the Postage Stamping technique (pg 44) to create panel out of chalk artwork.
5. Cut and mat artwork onto green cardstock; adhere to folded red card.
6. Stamp Happy Holidays in black ink along bottom of card.
7. Apply small amount of lacquer to berries and allow card to dry.

Peace Greeting

ROBEN-MARIE SMITH

MATERIALS

Rubber Stamps: Scripted Tree by Christine Adolph for Stampington & Co.; Peace by Wordsworth; Shadow Stamp by Just For Fun; Numbers by Postmodern Design

Pigment Inkpads: VersaFine (Onyx Black) by Tsukineko

Dye Inkpads: Adirondack (Denim) by Ranger

Papers: Navy Blue, Black and White Cardstock; Light Blue Cardstock by The Paper Cut

Embellishments: Black Gingham Ribbon; Black Photo Corners; Black Button

Adhesives: Glue Stick

Tools: Small Star Punch; Scissors; Paper Cutter

INSTRUCTIONS

1. Stamp Scripted Tree in Onyx Black onto white cardstock.
2. Ink Shadow Stamp in Denim and press over tree image.
3. Trim around image leaving only the tree and script.
4. Add photo corners to stamped panel and mat onto navy, light blue and black cardstock.
5. Cut and mat large piece of light blue cardstock onto folded black card; adhere stamped panel to card.
6. Stamp Peace and Numbers in black ink onto card as shown.
7. Tie black gingham ribbon around fold of card, creating bow in front. Pull ribbon ends through black button and knot in place.
8. Punch star from navy blue cardstock using star punch and adhere to top of tree.

TIPS
• Look for interesting pictures within your rubber stamps and experiment by using partial images.

Snowflake Trio

AMY WELLENSTEIN

TECHNIQUE
• Faux Watercolor with Marker and Dye Ink

MATERIALS

Rubber Stamps: Christmas Cube by Stampington & Co.

Dye Inkpads: Adirondack (Mountain Lake and Denim) by Ranger

Papers: Navy Blue and White Cardstock; Blue Patterned Paper by Paper Loft; Watercolor Paper

Embellishments: Merry Christmas Eyelet by Making Memories

Adhesives: Glue Stick

Tools: Embossing Heat Tool; Eyelet Setting Tool; 1/8" Hole Punch; Water Bottle; Paper Cutter

INSTRUCTIONS

1. Apply Mountain Lake and Denim inks to snowflake from Christmas Cube.
2. Lightly spritz inked stamp with water and press onto watercolor paper. Repeat this process twice and dry with heat tool.
3. Cut images to desired size and mat onto navy cardstock.
4. Adhere three stamped panels to blue patterned paper.
5. Cut and mat onto navy blue cardstock; adhere to folded white card.
6. Punch hole for eyelet placement and set Merry Christmas eyelet as shown.

St. Nicholas
ROBEN-MARIE SMITH

MATERIALS

Rubber Stamps: St. Nicholas by Carin Andersson for Stampington & Co.; Hope by Stampa Rosa

Dye Inkpads: StâzOn (Jet Black) by Tsukineko

Papers: Black and White Cardstock; Black Gingham and Red Patchwork Papers by K&Company; Green Patterned Paper by Carolee's Creations

Colored Pencils: Red and Green Watercolor

Embellishments: Black Index Tab by 7gypsies; White Button

Adhesives: Glue Stick; Tacky Glue; Glue Dots by Glue Dots International

Other: Small Bowl of Water

Tools: Embossing Heat Tool; Small Paintbrush; Scissors; Paper Cutter

TECHNIQUE
• *Highlight Coloring with Watercolor Pencils*

INSTRUCTIONS

1. Stamp St. Nicholas in Jet Black onto white cardstock.
2. Color image with watercolor pencils and lightly go over colors with wet paintbrush; dry with heat tool
3. Stamp Hope in black ink onto white cardstock and trim to fit inside folded index tab.
4. Cut St. Nicholas to desired size; fold index tab around image and glue in place.
5. Adhere panel onto Red Patchwork paper.
6. Cut and mat onto Green Patterned and Black Gingham papers. Tear Black Gingham paper along bottom and adhere panel to folded black card.
7. Attach button to index tab with Glue Dot.

TIPS
• Try coloring small areas of stamped images for a striking look.

Snowflake
ROBEN-MARIE SMITH

MATERIALS

Rubber Stamps: Snowflake Print by Christine Adolph for Stampington & Co.; Holiday Greetings by Wordsworth

Dye Inkpads: StâzOn (Jet Black) by Tsukineko

Papers: Green, Black and Textured Brown Cardstock; Red Patterned Paper by BasicGrey; Sheet Music

Embellishments: Black Photo Corners

Adhesives: Glue Stick

Tools: Scissors; Paper Cutter

TECHNIQUE
• *Collage with Stamps*

INSTRUCTIONS

1. Stamp Snowflake Print in Jet Black onto Red Patterned paper.
2. Cut and mat onto black cardstock and set aside.
3. Cut sheet music to desired size; attach photo corners and adhere to green cardstock.
4. Mat panel onto folded black card and attach original artwork in center.
5. Stamp Holiday Greetings in black ink onto textured brown cardstock.
6. Cut around image and adhere as shown.

Trust in the Lord

JILL HAGLUND

INSTRUCTIONS

Rubber Stamps: Trust in the Lord Phrase by Cheryl Darrow and Sara Crittendon for Uptown Rubber Stamps; Angel by DeNami Design; Large Swirl (unknown)

Pigment Inkpads: Encore! Ultimate Metallic (Gold) by Tsukineko

Dye Inkpads: Adirondack (Mountain Lake and Denim) by Ranger; StâzOn (Jet Black) by Tsukineko

Embossing Powders: Gold

Papers: Black, White and Glossy White Cardstock; Specialty Paper

Markers/Pens: Gold Leafing Pen by Krylon

Embellishments: Gold Ribbon

Adhesives: Glue Stick

Tools: Embossing Heat Tool; Scissors; Paper Cutter

MATERIALS

1. Rub Mountain Lake and Denim inks onto glossy white cardstock.
2. Stamp Large Swirl in Gold; apply embossing powder and emboss with heat tool.
3. Cut and mat onto black cardstock and specialty paper; adhere to folded white card.
4. Repeat step one and stamp Trust in the Lord Phrase and Angel over inked cardstock.
5. Cut out images separately and mat onto black cardstock.
6. Outline Angel panel in gold leafing pen; adhere inked panels to card as shown.
7. Tie gold ribbon around fold of card, creating bow in front.

Spiritus

JILL HAGLUND

MATERIALS

Rubber Stamps: Angel by JudiKins; Splatter by Diana Kovacs for Hampton Art Stamps; Spiritus (unknown); Background Script (unknown)

Pigment Inkpads: Encore! Ultimate Metallic (Gold) by Tsukineko; ColorBox Pigment (Royal Blue) by Clearsnap

Embossing Powders: Gold

Papers: Light Blue, Gold, and White Cardstock; Gold Tissue Paper; Specialty Paper

Pastels/Chalks: Yellow Chalk

Embellishments: Blue Tulle

Adhesives: Glue Stick; Tacky Glue; Adhesive Foam Tape

Other: Spray Fixative

Tools: Embossing Heat Tool; Cotton Swabs; Scissors; Paper Cutter

INSTRUCTIONS

1. Stamp Angel in Royal Blue onto white cardstock and set ink with heat tool.
2. Color image with yellow chalk using cotton swabs; spray with fixative and allow drying time.
3. Cut and mat image onto gold tissue paper, gold cardstock and specialty paper; adhere tulle and set panel aside.
4. Stamp Background Script in Gold onto gold cardstock; apply embossing powder and emboss with heat tool.
5. Stamp Background Script in Royal Blue onto light blue cardstock panel and color edge with ink.
6. Cut and mat stamped gold cardstock over stamped blue cardstock and set aside.
7. Stamp Splatter in Gold several times over folded blue card; apply embossing powder and emboss with heat tool.
8. Adhere script and angel panels onto card as shown.
9. Stamp Spiritus in Royal Blue onto light blue cardstock.
10. Cut out phrase and adhere to card with adhesive foam tape.

Angel in Prayer
JILL HAGLUND

MATERIALS

Rubber Stamps: Angel byJudiKins; Music by Stampington & Co.

Dye Inkpads: Adirondack (Mountain Lake) by Ranger; StâzOn (Jet Black) by Tsukineko

Papers: Black, White, Metallic Gold, and Glossy White Cardstock; Specialty Paper

Markers/Pens: Gold Leafing Pen by Krylon

Adhesives: Glue Stick

Other: Gold Webbing Spray by Krylon

Tools: Scissors; Paper Cutter

TECHNIQUES
- *Direct-to-Glossy Paper with Dye Ink*
- *Spray Webbing*

INSTRUCTIONS

1. Rub Mountain Lake ink onto glossy white cardstock and stamp Angel in Jet Black on top.
2. Cut and mat image onto black cardstock and specialty paper.
3. Outline Angel in gold leafing pen and set panel aside.
4. Ink additional glossy white cardstock in Mountain Lake ink along top and bottom.
5. Stamp Music in Jet Black in center and spray gold webbing over dye ink for textured look.
6. Cut and mat panel onto black and metallic gold cardstock.
7. Stamp Music in black ink onto folded white card and adhere stamped panels to card as shown.

Note: Angel in Prayer card is pictured on page 97.

Christmas Wreath
AMY WELLENSTEIN

MATERIALS

Rubber Stamps: Wreath and Berries by Christine Adolph for Stampington & Co.; Merry Christmas by Stampotique Originals

Pigment Inkpads: VersaMark Watermark (Clear) by Tsukineko

Dye Inkpads: Adirondack (Raisin) by Ranger; StâzOn (Jet Black) by Tsukineko

Papers: Red, Green, Black and Ivory Cardstock

Adhesives: Glue Stick; Diamond Glaze by JudiKins

Tools: Embossing Heat Tool; Paper Cutter

TECHNIQUE
- *Invisible Stamping*

INSTRUCTIONS

1. Stamp Wreath in Clear VersaMark onto green cardstock and set ink with heat tool.
2. Add Merry Christmas in black ink and Berries in Raisin to cardstock as shown.
3. Cut and mat artwork onto black and red cardstock; adhere to folded ivory card.
4. Apply small amount of Diamond Glaze to each berry and allow card to dry.

Pinecones
ROBEN-MARIE SMITH

MATERIALS

Rubber Stamps: Big Pinecone by Hero Arts; Postage Stamp by Limited Edition; Wishing You Phrase by Stampa Rosa

Dye Inkpads: Adirondack (Espresso) by Ranger

Papers: Gold and Brown Cardstock; Ledger Paper by K&Company

Adhesives: Glue Stick

Tools: Paper Cutter

TECHNIQUE
- *Collage with Stamps*

INSTRUCTIONS

1. Stamp Big Pinecone in Espresso ink onto Ledger paper.
2. Cut and mat image onto gold and brown cardstock and set aside.
3. Stamp pinecones on edge of large piece of Ledger Paper.
4. Cut and mat onto brown cardstock; adhere to folded gold card.
5. Stamp Wishing You Phrase and Postage Stamp in Espresso ink onto card as shown.

TIPS

- Webbing Spray comes in a variety of colors and adds interest and texture when used over stamped images or papers.

Wishing you a Beautiful Holiday Season

Merry Christmas

Wanted 4 Stolen Hearts

ROBEN-MARIE SMITH

TECHNIQUE
• *Collage with Stamps*

MATERIALS

Rubber Stamps: Mug Shot by Zettiology; Italian Text by Rubber Baby Buggy Bumpers; Criminal (unknown); Sqraffiti Alphabet by Stampotique Originals; Antique Alphabet by Hero Arts; Alphabet by Stamp Craft

Pigment Inkpads: VersaMagic Chalk Ink (Magnolia Bud) and VersaFine (Onyx Black) by Tsukineko

Dye Inkpads: Archival Ink (Sepia and Crimson) by Ranger

Papers: Red, Black and White Cardstock; Red Patterned Paper by Chatterbox

Embellishments: Large Tag

Adhesives: Glue Stick; Tacky Glue

Tools: Scissors; Paper Cutter

INSTRUCTIONS

1. Stamp Mug Shot in Onyx Black onto white cardstock.
2. Cut and mat image onto black cardstock as shown and adhere to tag.
3. Use various stamps from alphabet sets and stamp phrase in black ink.
4. Color edge of tag in Sepia for aged appearance and set aside.
5. Stamp Criminal in black ink onto red cardstock.
6. Stamp Italian Text in Magnolia Bud onto black cardstock.
7. Cut and mat red and black stamped cardstock over Red Patterned paper; adhere to folded black card.
8. Attach tag to card as shown.
9. Place your thumb in Crimson dye ink and press onto tag.

TIPS

• Use rubbing alcohol to remove dye ink from your skin.

Love is in the Air
AMY WELLENSTEIN

TECHNIQUE
- *Collage with Stamps*

MATERIALS

Rubber Stamps: Woman by The Moon Rose Art Stamps; Heart by Rubber Stampede; Script (unknown); Love Phrase (unknown)

Pigment Inkpads: VersaMark Watermark (Clear) by Tsukineko

Dye Inkpads: StâzOn (Jet Black) by Tsukineko

Embossing Powders: Ivory

Papers: Red, Black and Beige Cardstock

Adhesives: Glue Stick; Adhesive Foam Tape

Tools: Embossing Heat Tool; Scissors; Paper Cutter

INSTRUCTIONS

1. Stamp Heart in Clear Watermark several times over red cardstock.
2. Apply ivory embossing powder and emboss with heat tool.
3. Cut and mat onto small black cardstock panel; adhere to side of folded red card.
4. Stamp Script in Jet Black along opposite side.
5. Apply black ink to Woman stamp and press onto beige cardstock; cut out image.
6. Stamp Love Phrase in Clear Watermark in center of card; apply ivory embossing powder and emboss with heat tool.
7. Adhere Woman silhouette to card with adhesive foam tape.

Love Stamp Collage
JILL HAGLUND

TECHNIQUES
- *Paper Masking*
- *Collage with Stamps*

MATERIALS

Rubber Stamps: Forever and Always by Inkadinkado; The Kiss by Claudine Hellmuth for Stampington & Co.; Eros Ornamentum by Uptown Rubber Stamps; Small Swirl by A Stamp In The Hand; Love Block by Stampa Rosa; Postage Stamp (unknown)

Dye Inkpads: StâzOn (Jet Black) by Tsukineko; Adirondack (Cranberry) by Ranger

Papers: Heart-Shaped Card by Hero Arts

Embellishments: Red Ribbon; Gold Heart Charm

Adhesives: Tacky Glue

Other: Post-It® Notes or Removable Tape

Tools: Scissors

INSTRUCTIONS

1. Stamp Love Block in Cranberry in center of heart-shaped card.
2. Use the Paper Masking technique (pg 8) to hide image with Post-It® Notes.

3. Over stamp collage of images in black ink and remove mask when complete.
4. Tie red ribbon through gold heart charm and adhere to card as shown.

Be Mine
CAROLYN PEELER

Dye Inkpads: Tim Holtz Distress Ink (Tea Dye) by Ranger

Papers: White Cardstock; Donner (Red Striped) Paper by Melissa Frances; Definition Paper (unknown)

Embellishments: White Lace; Red Ribbon; Vintage Valentine Image

Adhesives: Glue Stick; Tacky Glue

Other: Red Craft Thread; Fine Pink Thread

Tools: X-ACTO™ Knife; Cutting Mat; Upholstery Needle; Sewing Machine; Scissors; Paper Cutter

TECHNIQUE
- *Collage with Ephemera*

INSTRUCTIONS

1. Cut and mat Donner paper to folded white card.
2. Wrap lace and definition paper around card front and adhere with tacky glue.
3. Color edge of vintage image with Tea Dye ink and adhere in center of card.
4. Thread upholstery needle with red craft thread and hand-stitch zigzag pattern over vintage image and lace as shown. Tie off thread in back.
5. Sew zigzag pattern along red ribbon with sewing machine using pink thread.
6. Cut small slit in fold of card near bottom using X-ACTO™ knife over cutting mat.
7. Wrap ribbon around bottom of card threading through the slit and tie in front.
8. Snip ribbon with scissors as shown.

TIPS
- Always consider adding a stamped message inside your card for a finishing touch.

XOXO Valentine
KELLY LUNCEFORD

MATERIALS

Rubber Stamps: Alphabet by Hero Arts; Floral Background by All Night Media

Pigment Inkpads: VersaMagic Chalk Ink (Cloud White) by Tsukineko

Dye Inkpads: StâzOn (Jet Black) by Tsukineko

Papers: Red and Black Cardstock

Embellishments: Playing Card; Vintage Fabric Image; Black Gingham Ribbon; Silver Metallic Thread

Adhesives: Glue Stick; Tacky Glue; Double-Sided Tape

Tools: 1/8" Hole Punch; Embossing Heat Tool; Scissors; Paper Cutter

TECHNIQUE
- *Collage with Ephemera*

INSTRUCTIONS

1. Stamp Floral Background in Cloud White onto front of folded red card and set with heat tool; edge card with black dye ink.
2. Cut small panel from black cardstock and punch hole in upper left-hand corner.
3. Tie black gingham ribbon and silver metallic thread through hole as shown.
4. Layer black cardstock panel, playing card and fabric fragment over card; adhere in place.
5. Stamp "XOXO" from Alphabet in black ink along bottom of card.

TIPS
- Glue will often show through fabric when used an adhesive. Double-sided tape works best.

Key to My Heart
JILL HAGLUND

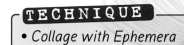

TECHNIQUE
- *Collage with Ephemera*

MATERIALS

Rubber Stamps: You've Got the Key to My Heart by Alias Smith & Rowe; The Kiss by Claudine Hellmuth for Stampington & Co.; Solid Spiral Heart by Uptown Rubber Stamps; Background Script by A Stamp In The Hand; Icon by Magenta; Love You by Stamp Francisco

Pigment Inkpads: Encore! Ultimate Metallic (Silver) by Tsukineko

Dye Inkpads: StâzOn (Jet Black) by Tsukineko

Embossing Powders: Silver

Papers: Black and White Cardstock; White Iridescent Paper

Embellishments: Pink Feathers; Silver Metallic Thread; Black and White Tulle; White Tag; Heart Rhinestone; Clear Bead

Adhesives: Glue Stick; Tacky Glue; Adhesive Foam Tape

Tools: Embossing Heat Tool; Scissors; Paper Cutter

INSTRUCTIONS

1. Stamp collage of images in black ink onto white cardstock.
2. Tear around images for textured look.
3. Stamp Background Script in Silver onto folded black card; apply embossing powder and emboss with heat tool.
4. Cut and adhere white iridescent paper to black card. Attach stamped paper with adhesive foam tape, layering tulle behind paper.
5. Lightly stamp Icon in black ink several times over tag; stamp Love You and tie silver metallic thread through top.
6. Adhere rhinestone heart and attach tag to card with adhesive foam tape.
7. Embellish card with feathers and clear bead as shown.

Prisoner of Love
KRISTY JEDINEK

TECHNIQUE
- *Collage with Ephemera*

MATERIALS

Rubber Stamps: Hearts (unknown); Floral Background (unknown)

Pigment Inkpads: Encore! Ultimate Metallic (Silver) by Tsukineko

Dye Inkpads: StâzOn (Blazing Red) by Tsukineko

Embossing Powders: Silver

Papers: Red, Black and White Cardstock

Embellishments: Silver Eyelet Snaps; Iridescent Thread; Silver and Letter Beads; Red Wire; Small White Envelope by Hero Arts

Tools: 1/8" Hole Punch; Embossing Heat Tool; Large Heart Punch; Eyelet Setting Tool; Wire Cutters; Scissors; Paper Cutter

INSTRUCTIONS

1. Stamp various heart images in Blazing Red onto white cardstock; cut and mat onto folded red card.
2. Stamp Floral Background in Silver onto red cardstock; apply embossing powder and emboss with heat tool.
3. Punch out two large hearts from embossed paper.
4. Wrap one heart in iridescent thread and tie off in back.
5. Cut off top of small white envelope. Stamp hearts in red ink on back of envelope and adhere to card as shown.
6. Adhere heart with thread to card, inserting bottom slightly inside envelope.
7. Cut small panel of black cardstock into strips and layer between second heart punch; adhere in place.
8. Punch holes for eyelet placement near bottom of card and set eyelets.
9. String red wire with silver and letter beads. Wrap ends of wire around eyelets.

Feathers, Ribbons & Things

JILL HAGLUND

MATERIALS

Pigment Inkpads: ColorBox MetalExtra (Goldrush) by Clearsnap

Papers: Purple and White Cardstock; Purple and White Corrugated Paper; Specialty Papers

Embellishments: Chipboard; Feathers; White, Purple and Speckled Tulle; Cloth Flower; Gold Ribbon; Metallic Gold Thread

Adhesives: Tacky Glue; E-6000 by Eclectic Products; Mod Podge Decoupage by Plaid

Tools: X-ACTO™ Knife; Cutting Mat; Small Foam Brush; Scissors; Paper Cutter

INSTRUCTIONS

1. Draw heart shape onto chipboard and cut out with X-ACTO™ knife over cutting mat.
2. Tear specialty papers into small strips, layer and decoupage over heart template; allow artwork to dry thoroughly.
3. Wrap heart in metallic gold thread as shown and tie in back.
4. Cut and mat purple cardstock and purple and white corrugated papers onto folded white card.
5. Layer gold ribbon and assorted tulle and adhere to card.
6. Attach heart and cloth flower to card with strong adhesive.
7. Add pink feathers for embellishment.

TIPS

• This is a great project for a class or group setting. Pass out heart templates to each person and place a bowl of assorted paper strips in the center of the table.

Love Collage

KRISTY JEDINECK

TECHNIQUES

• *Collage with Ephemera*
• *Transparencies on Top*

MATERIALS

Papers: Brown Cardstock; Text and Patterned Paper by 7gypsies; Script by K&Company

Embellishments: Transparency by K&Company; Love Button; Flower Photo

Adhesives: Glue Stick; Diamond Glaze by JudiKins

Tools: Scissors; Paper Cutter

INSTRUCTIONS

1. Cut and mat Patterned paper onto folded brown card.
2. Cut and tear papers and collage over Patterned paper.
3. Trim flower photo and adhere to card.
4. Cut definition from text paper and love transparency and adhere over collaged papers.
5. Attach love button to card as shown.

TIPS

• Love and heart-themed cards are perfect for every occasion including Mother's Day, Birthdays, Baby Showers, Anniversaries and Weddings.
• Photographs from magazines or old books make beautiful focal points.

Product Resource Guide

3M/Scotch: www.scotchbrand.com

7gypsies: www.7gypsies.com

A Stamp In The Hand: www.astampinthehand.com

Acey Deucy: retired company

Alias Smith & Rowe: www.asrstamps.com

All My Memories: www.allmymemoriesretailstore.com

All Night Media: www.plaidonline.com

American Art Clay Company: www.amaco.com

American Art Stamp: www.americanartstamp.com

A Muse Artstamps: www.amuseartstamps.com

Ann-ticipations: www.ann-ticipations.com

Anima Designs: www.animadesigns.com

Anna Griffin: www.annagriffin.com

ARTchix Studio: www.artchixstudio.com

Autumn Leaves: www.autumnleaves.com

B Line Designs, LLC: www.blinedesigns.com

BasicGrey: www.basicgrey.com

Bo-Bunny Press: www.bobunny.com

Canson: www.canson-us.com

Carolee's Creations: www.adornit.com

Catslife Press: www.catslifepress.com

CC Rubber Stamps: www.ccrubberstamps.com

Chatterbox, Inc.: www.chatterboxinc.com

Cherry Pie Art Stamps, LLC: www.cherrypieartstamps.com

Claudine Hellmuth: www.collageartist.com

Clearsnap, Inc.: www.clearsnap.com

Club Scrap: www.clubscrap.com

Collage Keepsakes: www.michaels.com

Daisy D's Paper Co.: www.daisydspaper.com

Delta Technical Coatings, Inc.: www.deltacrafts.com

DeNami Design: www.denamidesign.com

Design Originals: www.d-originals.com

Dove Brushes: www.dovebrushes.com

Eclectic Products: www.eclecticproducts.com

Elmer's Products, Inc.: www.xacto.com

Embossing Arts Co.: retired company

Fancifuls, Inc.: www.fancifulsinc.com

Fiskars Brands, Inc.: www.fiskars.com

Fred Mullett: www.fredbmullett.com

Glue Dots International, LLC: www.gluedots.com

Hampton Art, LLC: www.hamptonart.com

Hero Arts: www.heroarts.com

Hot Potatoes: www.hotpotatoes.com

Inkadinkado Rubber Stamps: www.inkadinkado.com

Just For Fun: www.jffstamps.com

K&Company: www.kandcompany.com

KI Memories: www.kimemories.com

Krylon: www.krylon.com

Li'l Davis Designs: www.lildavisdesigns.com

Limited Edition: www.limitededitionrs.com

Lucy Stamps: www.lucystamps.com.au

LuminArte, Inc.: www.luminarteinc.com

Lynne Perrella: www.stampington.com

Magenta: www.magentastyle.com

Magic Mesh: www.magicmesh.com

Making Memories: www.makingmemories.com

Marvy/Uchida of America Corp.: www.marvy.com

Melissa Frances: www.melissafrances.com

Nina Bagley: www.ninabagley.com

Paperbag Studios: www.paperbagstudios.com

Pebbles, Inc.: www.pebblesinc.com

Penny Black, Inc.: www.pennyblackinc.com

Personal Stamp Exchange (PSX):
www.sierra-enterprises.com

Picture Show: email:
pictureshowrubberstamps@msn.com

Plaid Enterprises, Inc.: www.plaidonline.com

Posh Impressions: www.poshimpressions.com

Post-it Notes/3M/Scotch: www.scotchbrand.com

Postmodern Design: 405-321-3176

PrintWorks Collection, Inc.:
www.printworkscollection.com

QuicKutz: www.quickutz.com

Ranger Industries, Inc.: www.rangerinc.com

Renaissance Art Stamps: 860-485-7761

Rio Grande: www.riogrande.com

River City Rubber Works:
www.rivercityrubberworks.com

Rubber Baby Buggy Bumpers: www.rubberbaby.com

Rubber Soul: www.rubbersoul.com

Rubber Stampede: www.rubberstampede.com

Rubbermoon Stamp Company:
www.rubbermoon.com

Rubberstamp Ave.: www.rubberstampave.com

Rusty Pickle: www.rustypickle.com

Sakura Hobby Craft: www.sakuracraft.com

Sarasota Stamps: retired company

Scrapbookpaper: www.scrapbookpaper.com

SonLight Impressions: retired company

Stamp Craft: www.stampcraft.com

Stamp Francisco: www.stampfrancisco.com

Stamp Out Cute: www.stamp-out-cute.com

Stampa Rosa: retired company

Stampendous: www.stampendous.com

Stampers Anonymous:
www.stampersanonymous.com

Stampin' Up!: www.stampinup.com

Stampington & Company: www.stampington.com

Stampotique Originals: www.stampotique.com

Tamp-A-Stamp: www.tamp-a-stamp.com

The Moon Rose: www.themoonroseartstamps.com

The Paper Cut: www.thepapercut.com

The Paper Loft: www.paperloft.com

Tin Can Mail: www.inkadinkado.com

Treasure Cay: www.eclecticmarketplace.com

Tsukineko: www.tsukineko.com

Unicorn Stempel: www.unicorn-stempel.de

Uptown Rubber Stamps/Uptown Design Company:
www.uptowndesign.com

Wordsworth: www.wordsworthstamps.com

X-ACTO/Elmer's Products: www.xacto.com

Zettiology: www.zettiology.com

Zig: www.eksuccess.com

Index of Techniques Used

TECHNIQUE INDEX

Look for Other How-to Books

from **TWEETYJILL PUBLICATIONS**

PAPERCRAFTING | STAMPING | GIFT IDEAS | ATCS

Scrapbook & Collage Papers ~The European Collection

A breath-takingly beautiful selection of 12" x 12" acid & lignin free papers: Italian marbled papers, French scripts and florals, exotic ephemera and vintage-style coffee-dyed paper. Available also as companion to Vintage Collage for Scrapbooking.
Retail $24.95 • 80 pgs • 89812

Vintage Collage for Scrapbooking

Tons of ideas for using vintage materials and products to create a family history album! Step-by-step photos, materials list and detailed instruction for each page layout. Papers and Ephemera used throughout this title are available in Scrapbook & Collage Papers~The European Collection.
$21.95 • 112 pgs • 89805

Making Cards with Rubber Stamps, Ribbons & Buttons

Card projects for all skill levels featuring rubber stamps, ribbon snippets, bright colored inkpads, buttons and tulle. Beautiful photos of every project!
$21.95 • 128 pgs • 89808

Creating Vintage Cards

Make cards using your vintage photos. Sassy to sophisticated and whimsical to elegant card ideas. High quality designs explained in easy step-by-step directions.
$21.95 • 112 pgs • 89806

Shabby & Beyond Scrapbooking Ideas

Ribbons, silk flowers, papers, brads, buttons, fabrics, fibers and trims mingle with transparencies, rub-ons, alphabet stamps, paints, distressed tags, inks and imaginative fonts. The must-have idea book!
Retail $24.95
176 pgs • 89809

Great Gift Ideas using Scrapbook Materials

Use scrapbook papers and embellishments to create one-of-a-kind gifts. Materials, simple instructions and illustrative photos for each idea.
Retail $21.95
112 pgs • 89810

Artists Creating with Photos

Well-known artists' journals, cards, boxes, blocks, scrapbook layouts, clipboards, frames and assemblages. Beautiful photography and simple instructions.
Retail $21.95
112 pgs • 89807

Rubber Stamping Artist Trading Cards (ATCs)

Discover ATCs with a twist – ours are mostly done with ink and rubber stamp images (with some embellishments) Join the fun and get in on the ATC craze!
Retail $24.95
160 pgs • 89811

Creating with Fabric

Make the move from paper to fabric! Learn and be inspired by well-known international artists such as KC Willis, Lesley Riley, Lisa Engelbrecht, Pamela Allen, Julie McCullough, Jill Haglund and more. Includes steps and photos to make fabric treasures.
Retail $21.95 • 112 pages • 89813

ALTERED! Art Projects

A must-have collection of altered art projects! Featured in this book are: birdhouses, shadowboxes, windowpanes, wood hearts, bowls, framed collages, scrapbook pages, boxes, and much more. Page after page of talent and fabulous art...one hot title!
Retail $21.95 • 112 pages • 89814

Tweety Jill
PUBLICATIONS
makes you creative!

You can find these and other TweetyJill books at your local bookseller, or order by calling: **1.800.595.5497.** Visit us at: **www.tweetyjill.com**
5824 Bee Ridge Rd. • PMB 412 • Sarasota, FL 34233